The Messenger of Machu Picchu

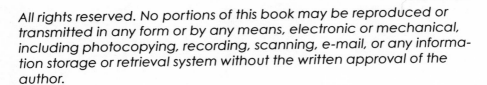

This book is a reflection of my own spiritual understandings and is not intended to speak for any spiritual path, teacher, or religion. In this book I have made occasional use of certain terms (Eckankar, Soul Travel, and Mahanta) that are trademarks of Eckankar. This does not imply any endorsement or sponsorship by Eckankar. I have intended only to make a fair use of such terms, recognizing that the rights to their trademark usage belong entirely to Eckankar.

The characters, organizations and events portrayed in this novel are either the products of the author's imagination or are used fictionally. The characters are fictional and any similarity to those living or deceased is purely coincidental.

Printed in the USA

Edited by Debbie Johnson

Library of Congress Cataloging-in-Publication Data

Switzer, Bob

The Messenger of Machu Picchu, A Spiritual Adventure

Library of Congress Control Number: 2011904583

Spirituality, Spiritual Life, Personal Growth, Self Help

ISBN: 1-4610-1223-6
ISBN-13: 9781461012238

*High in the Andes Mountains of Peru, a gripping adventure of romance
and spiritual awakening unfolds revealing sacred wisdom that has
the power to change people's lives forever.*

The Messenger of Machu Picchu

A Spiritual Adventure

Bob Switzer

Dedication

For

Seekers of wisdom everywhere
and to
Sri Harold Klemp,
the Mahanta, the Living ECK Master
my spiritual guide and teacher,
and to Andrea,
for sharing the challenge of a lifetime in Peru
in recording this story, and for making
our life together an ongoing adventure.

Table of Contents

Acknowledgement

With special thanks to prom peru
in helping me visit Peru and trek the Inca Trail
enabling me to enrich the story
with some incredible personal experiences.

Preface

What is Being Spiritual?

This interesting question was posed to me by a friend and gave me much cause for thought. After contemplating the subject I've decided that being spiritual for me is about bringing God-like qualities into my life. It is interrelating or treating others with spiritual qualities present such as compassion, respect, grace, forgiveness, honesty, humility and more. It's being a force for love, harmony, humor and joy to those around me. I've learned as well that if we want any quality in our life, we must become that quality and give it to others. Like attracts like.

The key to my spiritual growth over the past thirty years—bringing spiritual qualities into my way of being and gaining the benefits—has been my daily contemplation routine, just like Jack, the main character in The Messenger of Machu Picchu. My contemplations are now part of my work and integral to my enjoyment of life, and the benefits have been enormous. I see life from a different perspective. Like Jack, I see meaning in dreams, coincidences, déjà-vu experiences, intuitions and nudges, experiences with light and sound, the appearances of animals and other forms of nature, and I recognize these are all working for my greater good. Life is guided. Decisions become conscious choices. Pitfalls, danger and troubles can be avoided. And an inner confidence develops and leads to contentment and joy.

Recognition of this guidance is the first step. Trusting our spiritual signals is the next, and daily contemplation, what I call a spiritual exercise is the key. It helps one develop spiritual attunement and gives one the spiritual strength to trust the signs Spirit provides—gut feelings, how the heart is responding to situations, in addition to those previously mentioned. I would define this process as awakening spiritually.

I've discovered there is an inherent relationship in spiritual growth, between giving and receiving. The more one gives (spiritual qualities), the more one receives in the way of spiritual gifts (guidance, intuition etc.), that can help us go through life in a much smoother, graceful way.

Being a giving being with spiritual qualities present opens the heart, the gateway to Soul, creating a greater receptivity and trust of the guidance provided by Spirit.

It has taken many years and an adventure in Peru to infuse my personal experiences into the story to ready the book for your enjoyment and hopefully confirm for you many spiritual truths that are already in your heart.

In the spirit of adventure....

Bob Switzer

Chapter 1
Hearing Spirit's Call

<u>August 30</u>

Climbing to cruising altitude over the Atlantic, I flipped down my tray table as the captain switched off the seat-belt light and pulled the battered journal out of my carry-on bag at my feet. The last few weeks had been the most action-packed days of my life and the next six hours to London seemed like the best time of any to refresh my memory and make some additional notes if I was ever going to share what happened with anyone. I pushed my seat back all the way, closed my eyes and thought to myself that I'd better just start from the beginning.

"It's amazing what can happen if you ask," I mused, "but one definitely needs to be open to change and up for adventure."

I decided to start with the day everything began to shift. Opening my eyes for a second, I checked the date of that entry. It was July 28.

Here is how it all began, how my life shifted one hundred and eighty degrees; physically, emotionally, mentally, spiritually—totally!

<u>July 28</u>

As I awoke the voice said, "*You will find the secret, wrapped in an enigma, found within a mystery.*" Scratching my head, these words echoed in my subconscious, all

2

I could remember of the dream I'd just had along with a vague image of a strange man. I reached over to my bedside table, grabbed my journal, and with my eyes half open made a rudimentary drawing of the crude mountain hut made of stone on the steep slope, and the odd looking man dressed in a robe reminiscent of ancient times, and everything else that I could remember. My normal daily entries made a little more sense than this one, I thought, but perhaps this dream would reveal its meaning in time.

As I got out of bed and glanced out my window, I could see it was another hot and humid St. Louis morning. Looking over the urban scene through my almost floor to ceiling windows on the thirty-third floor, there was a mist draped over the streets and buildings and the breaking sun was just starting to burn off the haze to reveal the cityscape at five-thirty in the morning. I walked over to my notebook computer, pressed the space bar to wake it up and clicked on to our site. I wanted to check the London market which was in full swing and sure enough, it was already up twenty points due to the news of the mega-merger of two global banking giants. I thought to myself that at least half of my clients would do well, the ones that trusted me and listened.

I was still in my pajamas when I sat down and began to relax as I did every morning. This particular morning, I thought I would sit in the bedroom to do my contemplation, what I came to know as a spiritual exercise, something I had been doing for the last five years since developing an ulcer. I got relaxed and began to chant HU, (which sounds like the man's name Hugh) an ancient mantra. I used to contemplate with the sound of Om, the first sound that I learned, but three years ago my friend Joyce had suggested using "HU" which she said is chanted or sung by many people in different cultures around the world. She had told me it was an ancient name for God and the sound could be compared to white light that contains all colors, because the HU sound contains all sounds of the universe. She had also let me know that singing HU helps one align with the higher vibratory rates of the spiritual worlds and of the Creator. And so with practice I have found it to be a very powerful sound for me, carrying me to deep levels of relaxation, clarity and insights. That morning, like all others, I started singing HU with all my heart, like a love song to God. My practice was to sing HU in a long drawn-out breath like HUUUUUUU. As I settled into my chant I thought that others would hear me in the condo units above and below in the quiet of the morning, but then I pondered, if the sound carried that far it would only sound like the wind or some other sound of nature anyway.

Over the last few years I had become a different person, thank God. In the earlier part of my life I was really an animal, a selfish, unconsciousness being. As I drifted deeper into contemplation I was feeling how things are different today. Life is now so authentic, I reflected, working in harmony with Spirit. As I sang HU, I began to have a strong feeling I was ready for more, to work more with Spirit.

I had found that the key is listening. Every morning I would do my spiritual exercise, and as part of this practice, I'd ask Spirit what I could do to serve It. And the answers would come. It wasn't always this way, though. I had to work at it for these last few years. But then the inner sound came like a rush of water, and then I began to hear a high-pitched electrical sound. On occasion I also could hear a field of crickets. My friend Joyce had told me that the inner sounds of Spirit can manifest as many different sounds like bells, rushing water, the buzzing of bees, chimes and even like the sound of bagpipes in the distance.

One day two winters before, the most amazing thing had happened. I was shoveling snow at my dad's place and I began to see a blue light. When I had closed my eyes it got even brighter, and all I could do was stand there and look with my eyes closed at this amazing blue light. It was electric sky blue and was shaped like a sort of blob with a golden corona around it like an eclipse of the sun. This light stayed with me for about a minute and a half and then gradually began to fade. I realized this is what Joyce and some of her friends were talking about when they said to look for the light when they were singing HU. What an amazing experience it was!

I was thinking about this experience as I sat there singing quietly now. The waves of peace began to roll over me and the sound began to ring louder in my inner hearing. My life, it seemed, had been getting boring, and I was feeling stale and empty but I knew that I had to take responsibility for creating what I wanted in life. I had the realization a few years ago that I am the master of my life; that I have to create it. And so as I chanted I asked Spirit, What's next? What can I do?

The brokerage experience was good for me, especially financially, but I was beginning to feel hollow. I guess "unfulfilled" would be the best way to describe it. I wanted more from life, but I could not define what that "more" was, yet I had the strong sense that there was more to experience. I had felt inner nudges before, but some of them were so hard to go with. The nudges and feelings, if followed, would have meant leaving my job and moving, and I had lived in St. Louis all my life. My family was there and so were all my friends, many from high school that I saw often. But I had this feeling building inside of me that I needed to change.

Continuing my inner reflection, I could feel the deep relaxation set in and I knew that I was off to the inner worlds. The key was to stay alert so that I could remember the experiences and bring them back to my waking state. The light was getting brighter and the inner sounds held my attention as I could faintly hear the sound of chimes as well as the high pitched electrical sound that I almost always heard now while doing my spiritual exercises and even when I was going about my day if I placed my attention on it.

My attention was drawn to a vision that was beginning to appear and I began to perceive high mountain peaks and ancient ruins. I was there again, I thought! Three times in the last week I had seen glimpses of the ancient city that I now recognized as Machu Picchu in Peru, having seen it on a Discovery Channel show a few weeks back. I had developed a fascination for Peru and this experience brought it all back into focus. The scene was getting clearer with a sky almost the electric blue of the inner light that I had seen on those previous occasions. The sun was rising and there was a mist burning off in the morning sun, mirroring the scene I had observed as I looked outside my condo just a few minutes ago. The vista was so stirring, I felt that I belonged there.

As the scene unfolded, I sensed myself high up, looking down on the ancient tableau, and then a face appeared. The face of someone familiar was superimposed over the vision, yet I could not place him. He didn't look like he was from this area of the world—he had jet black wavy hair, combed straight back, and a face with chiseled features including a large square nose, a high broad forehead and an expansive smile revealing large pure white teeth. In general, his appearance was from a culture that I had never seen before.

The face faded and I was left with the setting in the mountains, then that also slowly receded. As I began to come out of my spiritual exercise, I thought aloud that this was the third time I'd been there in the inner worlds of my contemplations in the last week or so. But this was the first time I had seen the face. I opened my eyes and took a deep breath. I reached for my journal on the side table and made a note of the experience for a few minutes. I felt totally relaxed and ready for another busy day of trading and constant contact with clients on the telephone but I had a deep feeling that I was going to see some changes too.

The day went well with clients calling me, thanking me for my advice on the bank stock purchase and asking how long they should hold it. As usual, I left the office at six p.m. and headed down the street with my radio in my ear listening to my favorite call-in show. That evening the host was asking for callers to share their experiences with their dreams, specifically, dreams where they were given a look at the future. There was a lady who called to relate the story of her cat having a litter of kittens, all white except one that was all black, and the dream she had had three months earlier about the same thing happening. The second caller was a lawyer telling about his dream about his friend being accused of murder and having to defend him, and that it had come true. And then a man called in about his dream about Machu Picchu. My heart stopped! There was that place again! It brought back the total experience from my morning contemplation as I slowed my pace. This was no coincidence, I rationalized. Three spiritual exercises with the same experience, and now a caller on a radio show. "What are the odds?" I thought. As of the last year, I knew better than to doubt. I knew in that moment that there was something that I had to do, but what? Go there?

As I continued walking, the familiar ringing of my spiritual exercises started in my ears. I had no sooner hatched the idea about going to Machu Picchu, when the ringing started. I thought, wow! This would be a change. I had traveled to California to climb Mount Baldy, to Florida to explore the Everglades, and to Arizona to do white water rafting in the Grand Canyon, but I had never been outside of the USA. Stopping to pull the earphone out of my ear I listened to the sound. In spite of the sounds of traffic, it was still there. I immediately felt like it was a message to me that I was connecting with that insight about Machu Picchu—that I was in harmony with it.

I looked up and down the street and found I was standing outside the Flight Center! Side-stepping through other pedestrians hurrying along the sidewalk, I moved over to the sign in the window and saw they had listed destinations and prices to all the major cities around the word. And there under the L's was Lima, and a special fare of five hundred and ninety-nine dollars. I was immediately drawn inside as I reached for the door handle, opened the door and walked inside. It had been a year since I'd taken a holiday and the office encouraged us to take our vacation in the summer when most clients took their holidays. But I also had no idea when would be the best time to travel to Peru.

I walked up to the first desk where an agent had just finished putting down the phone. She looked up at me, smiled and invited me to sit down. Reaching out her hand, she introduced herself as Marina with a lilting Latin accent. I shook her hand and eased into the chair in front of her desk.

She smiled and asked, "How can I help you?" She had beautiful brown polished skin and sparkling dark eyes be-

8

hind her rectangular high fashion glasses. Her long jet-black hair with a few white strands was pulled back into a long pony tail.

I replied, *"I would like to ask about flights to Lima. I'm fascinated with Machu Picchu."*

She immediately became animated and I could tell she was excited about the area. She explained how she'd been born in Bolivia, a neighboring country to Peru and had traveled to Peru and visited Machu Picchu on three occasions as a young woman with her family. She said she had wonderful memories of the trips. After ten minutes of listening to her stories about Peru and Machu Picchu, her feelings were contagious and I could hardly contain the enthusiasm building inside me. I knew this was what I needed to do. I was feeling excited and connected; it felt very right and so I pulled out my cell phone and made a call to Jim, my branch manager. Luckily he was still at the office and was able to give me the all clear to leave in two weeks.

Half an hour later, I left the travel agency with ticket in hand and a strange feeling that my life was going to change, but I was also excited, like an adventure was just beginning. Everything had connected so fast and effortlessly. I was used to spiritual adventures, traveling in my contemplations to the inner worlds, but this was a whole new ball game!

When I got home, my first thought was to call Roger, my traveling buddy, and invite him to come too, but it didn't feel right. When I had reached for the telephone, I had to put it down. Somehow I knew I needed to do this trip on my own. This was my adventure. I'd learned a few years ago that I needed to follow my inner nudges and to trust them and this one felt very natural to follow. But life is a constant test in this regard, and I tend to think too much sometimes. In the end, I have learned to trust my nudges and my experiences that talk to me. And as life would have it, I remembered I had received a validation; the man that had called the radio station told the host about his Machu Picchu dream. The man he described was my man too! It was as if his words were describing the man that I had seen in my contemplation that morning!

Chapter 2
The Master Appears

Two weeks later I flew American Airlines from St. Louis to Miami and then connected to Lima. The flight took four and a half hours from Miami and was smooth and uneventful, although I felt the on-board movie was preparing me for the experience I was about to have. In the classic movie, *The Family Man*, Nicholas Cage was given a preview of what his life would have been like had he followed his heart and stayed with his college sweetheart. Instead, he went into the brokerage business in London and followed the money and his mind. It made me think about changes I had made and the events that were taking me to Peru.

Lima airport felt small for the city size of eight million. On disembarking the plane, the immigration hall was jammed. Forty-five minutes later I was stamped through immigration and discovered that the timing was perfect as the luggage belt had just started up. My bags were at the end, but soon I was on my way by taxi to San Isidro, a downtown section of Lima.

The area departing the airport looked rough around the edges but as we drove closer to the center of Lima, the cityscape of low-lying strip-mall style buildings improved from rough to not-so-rough. The outskirts of Lima actually felt a lot like parts of Los Angeles that I remembered, only without the freeways. Then we entered the district of San Isidro, and I began to feel at home with the cleanliness and neatness of Lima's downtown. We passed majestic buildings that were four and five stories tall, cast in a pale yellow cement-stucco exterior. The architecture was impressive, Spanish colonial, with arches and pillars common to many buildings. We drove through two plazas with statues and fountains, and past bustling shopping districts, then entered an area of quiet streets lined with parked cars and more trees. It was dusk when the taxi came to an abrupt stop, and I could see I had arrived at a small intimate hotel in a somewhat residential neighborhood. Over the entrance doors to the building were the words, "Sonesta Posada del Inca"

I paid the cabby the agreed fifteen dollars for the ride and a couple of bucks extra for a tip as he set my bag near the reception desk. The petite receptionist greeted me with a smile in Spanish and I replied in English. She quickly switched to English and I was checked in efficiently and I followed the porter to my room on the third floor. He opened the door for me and then followed me into the room, turning on lights as he passed switches. He went immediately to the television and turned it on as though this was the most important feature of the hotel. Then he showed me how to open the window. He turned to me with a big smile and said, "*Please to hope you have good stay in Lima.*" I smiled and wearily said, "Thanks," and pressed a dollar bill into his hand. He appeared very grateful and made his exit as I put my bag on the dresser.

I was excited and tired at the same time. Fatigue was hitting me hard, and I had an early flight from Lima on the coast to Cusco high in the Andes Mountains in the morning, so I abandoned plans to scout around the city that evening in favor of sleep. I got undressed, threw my clothes over a chair and climbed into bed. I leaned over to the phone, dialed zero and asked for a six a.m. wake-up call and then put my head on the pillow. Sleep came fast as I sang HU two or three times to relax me completely before drifting off.

August 11

I'm ascending a moderately steep trail. My left hand holds hers with a grip of relaxed familiarity. Concern flows through my body as the mountain peaks are now catching the morning light. The two of us press on, more relaxed now but still not out of danger.

My heart still pounds from the earlier panic but as I catch a sideways glance at my trail-mate, my heart leaps at the vision of beauty I perceive with platinum strands of her hair dazzling around her face, caught in the dawning light. The silence of the cool mountain air is inexplicably disturbed by a distant throb which drifts into my awareness. She hears it too! It fades away and we press on. Momentarily, the throbbing sound returns, now more evident, dissolving in and out of our hearing.
"I know that sound," she says. "I just can't place it."
"Me too," I respond. "Let's keep moving," as the urgency in my step increases.

The vegetation is now getting thinner affording us less cover. I anxiously look behind for any signs of pursuit, but we appear to be alone on the mountain. I am puffing again and so is she. Apprehension is now beginning to overtake our briefly won calm of a few minutes ago.

14

Suddenly an explosion just out of sight over a rise jolts me out of the experience and I find myself awake.

Feeling clammy with sweat I lay there for a few moments but soon I am drifting back into the lucid dream.

We are still together, the beautiful woman and I, yet I sense she is behind me. I am floating in a canoe. My vision is gone. Blackness pervades as I intuit we are floating along in a relative calm. Nothing to see, just experience the void, trusting all will work out. I realize I am chanting—the sound is what is giving me the inner trust, the knowingness of protection. We float along.

The sound is now louder and I realize I am waking up, still softly chanting.

Lying in bed, my eyes began to adjust to the light illuminating the inside of my eyelids.

"What was that about?" I question myself silently.

As I laid there in my half-waking state, I reviewed the details. Was it a dream? If felt so real! I mentally recaptured the light, the sounds, the memory of her, and my feelings for her. Yes, love. Pure love like I have never known.

Reaching for my dream journal on the bedside table I began writing. Fifteen minutes later, I finished recording, and the vivid events have become a part of my memories as I lay there lost in a reflective reverie.

The phone rang, jolting me fully awake and at the second ring I realized that it was my wake-up call. After showering, shaving and dressing I went down to the cafe off the lobby for some breakfast that was included in the price of the room. I helped myself to an excellent buffet of eggs, bacon, cold meats, cereals, breads and strong black coffee. On the way back to the room I asked for a taxi and the receptionist pointed to a line of several cabs waiting out front. With transportation solved, I went back to my room and put my toiletries back into my bag which was still packed from the night before, and went back down to check out. Within minutes I was seated in the back of a small Toyota taxi headed back to Lima's airport.

The coastal city was very hazy as the taxi sped along at just after seven a.m. to the airport for my one hour flight to Cusco, situated to the southeast and perched at eleven thousand feet, high in the Andes. Traffic was very light and I didn't see any speed limit signs. Red lights didn't seem to matter to the cabby either, and my concern grew after we drove straight through the first red light. But the taxi driver would slow to about forty miles per hour, look and then continue as did the rest of the traffic at certain red lights. Railroad crossings were identified by two continuous red flashing lights which gave me additional cause for concern, to put it mildly. The first couple of crossings passed before I realized the flashing lights are on all the time at the major crossings in Lima. I was still hoping for no more red traffic lights all the way to the airport, but we managed to blast through four more on the way!

I arrived at the airport in one piece, but my heart was racing and it wasn't just from the Peruvian coffee! My check-in was efficient and within the hour I was airborne in the Boeing 737 climbing over the rough dry terrain to the east of Lima. As we flew north- east toward Cusco, the clear view of the exceptionally dry and jagged coastal mountain range below gave way to cloud cover with the odd glimpse of a snowy peak just a short distance below, which told me we were now flying over the high Andes Mountains.

Within fifty minutes we had begun our descent into Cusco one of the world's highest cities. Looking out the window I could clearly see it nestled in a narrow green valley. It actually looked like a small town, which it turned out to be from a traveler's perspective, and seemed quaint looking with all the red-tiled rooftops. We flew up the valley passing almost directly over the town between two mountain ranges, and then the aircraft banked sharply around two low peaks, completing a one hundred and eighty degree turn. Within less than a minute we were on the ground at over eleven thousand, three hundred feet above sea level.

Cusco airport seemed larger than Lima's and definitely more beautiful. A local ensemble was playing Peruvian music and for the first time I really felt like I was in the Peru I wanted to experience, listening to the distinct pan flute sounds of the region. A porter and then a taxi driver found me right away and soon I was riding gently to the center of town in moderate traffic, a sharp contrast to the ride and pace of Lima. I was dropped off in front of my hotel, an old colonial building, and walked inside through a covered portico with pillars. It was another Posada del Inca hotel, a local Peruvian chain, and situated just off the main square of the town.

Upon checking in with reception, to my delight, my room was already available adding to my feelings of synchronisity. The porter showed me up to the third floor of the six story hotel. We walked all the way down the hall to the end and the porter opened the door and led me into a corner room, a bonus. He went to the far window and opened it inviting me to look out at the view of the old colonial town and its beautiful architecture. I gazed at the main square surrounded by beautiful old Spanish style buildings with colonial architecture while the perfect seventy degree air freshened up the room. He then led me over to the other window and opened it as well. Looking out in this direction I could see red-tiled roof tops and mountain peaks behind. The porter then left after telling me the breakfast service would be shutting down in ten minutes on the top floor in the roof garden cafe.

I felt a little light-headed at the high altitude, but I had come prepared with a homeopathic remedy for altitude headaches that I had bought in St. Louis, having followed an inner nudge to get some at the local health food store before leaving. I reached into my bag and pulled out the tiny bottle and put another drop on my tongue. Fortunately I had started taking the remedy a few days before the trip. I lay down on the bed to relax for a while and I thought to myself, "What next?" In a flash, the answer came. It was time for my spiritual exercise, as I had not done it upon rising in Lima. This is how I had been tuning in each day to what Spirit would like me to do and was determined to keep my good habit intact. My spiritual exercises had become an important part of my life; it was the most efficient way to start my day, by asking what I should do. In effect, the practice had become my time to tune into my highest perspective, Soul, to determine the flow for the day. After these last few years, I'd found that going with the flow was the most joyful and efficient way to move through the day and enjoy life.

As I lay there, I began as usual with HU and sang this ancient word until the street sounds that were drifting in through the windows began to fade into the recesses of my consciousness. And then I shifted to my new sound that had come to me a few weeks ago when I asked Spirit for help in rejuvenating my contemplation experiences. I had learned not only do I have to constantly take responsibility to create my outer life, but that I need to take the same approach with my inner life as well.

I began to hear the inner sound, the high pitched electrical sound that I had become used to, and then a new sound began to enter my awareness. It sounded like the single note of a flute. As I began to listen and enjoy this sound, a picture began to form in my head. I could see myself up in the mountains again but this time, sitting in the doorway of a hut. In the valley below I could see Machu Picchu. And then the scene faded. I continued with my Spiritual exercise for another fifteen minutes wondering about the scene and resolved to make my way to the ancient city tomorrow as my excitement continued to build. Somehow I knew the journey was going to have a special meaning for me.

When I finished my spiritual exercise, I decided to do some light exploring in the Cusco area, the old imperial Inca capital which was both the administrative and religious center of the empire. I felt like doing something not too strenuous the first day at over eleven thousand feet, and so I spoke to the smiling ladies at the hotel reception. I wanted to set my own pace and they recommended that I hire a taxi for the afternoon to see the sites. Out on the street I talked to the first taxi in line and he spoke a little English. His name was Eduardo and he told me for just forty soles, about fifteen dollars, he would take me to four ancient sites that I could explore on my own. I thought, at that price it was a no-brainer.

He drove for about five minutes out of the town center and we arrived at the first stop, Saccayhuaman. Reading the brochure I picked up in the hotel lobby, I discovered that it was an Inca military fortress built to protect Cusco, a mile and a bit north of town. The fortress was built on enormous polished rocks in a saw-tooth shape. Standing on one, I could look down on Cusco with its red-tiled rooftops and narrow cobbled streets. I spent a half hour exploring the ancient ruins of the fort walls that zigzagged along the ridge and the high plain, then Eduardo waved at me and I knew it was time to move on.

Next, Eduardo drove me to Tambomachay, old Inca baths and a resting place for Inca monarchs, where I climbed the ancient ruins. I was so impressed with the scene that I sat down did a ten minute spiritual exercise with the sun at my back and the wind in my face. It was one of those special moments you want to savor and keep for future times when someone asks you to think of a truly beautiful and peaceful place as part of a personal growth workshop exercise. After about forty five minutes at Saccayhuaman, Eduardo gave me the signal again, waving at me from the car and I knew it was time to move on.

Following the narrow winding roads surrounding Cusco, we headed for Kenko, a ritual site consisting of a circular amphitheater and labyrinth. I was able to explore the very old underground galleries for a half hour. On the last stop, Eduardo took me to Puca Pucara, meaning "the red fortress" in the Quechua language, once part of Cusco's capital defense system. This structure was comprised of terraces, stairways, dungeons and windows. There I was able to sit with the afternoon sun and mild wind in my face, drinking in the valley and the mountains behind. An hour later, we headed back to the town center and the hotel.

After another late afternoon nap in my room, I set out to find a place to eat. As I left the Posada del Inca hotel, I headed up the street toward the main square. It was getting dark, and to my surprise the old colonial cathedrals and other buildings were beautifully illuminated in golden floodlights, and the streets were alive with people. Many wore brightly colored hats, jackets and pants. One lady with an orange embroidered head piece passed me carrying the cutest little new born baby llama in her arms. She was also carrying her tiny baby on her back in a papoose made of rainbow colored striped cloth. Everywhere the locals were smiling, and I noticed that they had a very gentle nature about them. Even the odd street merchant selling postcards or jewelry was not as persistent as I'd expected. I noticed that when I smiled, they were very graceful. However, when I responded with firmness, they were equally as persistent. This was an interesting reflection for me in that I received back exactly what I gave out.

I explored the narrow cobbled streets which, to my delight, were lined with small boutique restaurants, as well as tour and trekking companies, trekking outfitters, and stores and merchant stalls selling every craft you could imagine from hats, alpaca sweaters and ponchos, to beautiful hand-made native Quechua jewelry. I decided to browse and save any buying for the markets near Machu Picchu. I had heard that the natives travel for over a day to get to the market there to sell their crafts, although even in the center of Cusco the merchandise was a bargain by American standards.

Everywhere, street sales representatives with menus in hand were anxious to introduce me to their restaurant. After being approached several times with requests to review their menus, I ended up in a tiny bistro off the main square. It turned out to be one of the best meals I've ever had; fresh caught trout served Peruvian style, grilled with herbed butter. Overall, the dining in Cusco turned out to be an amazing surprise and I read later that according to the food critics the cuisine in Cusco was on par with other world class centers such as New Orleans, Quebec City and Cannes. And I would agree. Even the pizza was great!

After dinner, the streets were even busier as the locals came out to enjoy the town's late night shopping, dining and night-life activities. The town center was now totally aglow in the golden light of the illuminations of the architectural facades around the several town squares. I enjoyed a pleasant stroll back to the hotel along the tiny cobbled streets and walkways, many that were covered and lined with arched pillars, part of the buildings that lined each square. When I got back to my hotel room I went to bed early, around nine p.m., excited about catching the first train to Machu Picchu in the morning.

August 12

My wake-up call got me up with the rising sun reflecting off the red tiled rooftops out my east-facing window. After a shower, shave and short contemplation, I found the breakfast room on the roof garden and helped myself to the all-inclusive great buffet breakfast and black coffee. I was really beginning to like Peru! After a swift check-out, I jumped in a waiting taxi out front. The ride to the train station was pleasantly unhurried and I was able to get a ticket on the seven a.m. special, which offered a slightly lower price than the more popular eight a.m. departure that most tourists took.

On pulling out of the station I decided to use the time to make a couple of journal entries, and I noted seeing Machu Picchu in my Spiritual exercise yesterday as well as all the sights in Cusco. As we chugged along, I discovered that we were actually headed downhill into the Sacred Valley of the Incas, the site of many ancient and spectacular Inca ruins and after about an hour, I could see we were following the banks of the Urubamba River, which flows from the Cusco region and empties hundreds of miles later into the interior reaches of the Amazon River in Brazil. I later learned that we had descended to about nine thousand two hundred feet from Cusco's eleven thousand three hundred feet.

We passed by Ollantaytambo, an extensive Inca archeological town site that we could see from the train. Reading another brochure, I learned that Ollantaytambo was a typical Inca community and was named in honor of the chief Ollanta who was famous for courting an Inca princess, daughter of Pachutec. One of the best preserved areas, the Andean Terraces, could be seen from the train window on the imposing hillside as we slowly moved past. Also visible were archeological structures including the Temple of the Sun and the Manacaray or Royal Hall.

We then continued to follow the Rio Urubamba, passing through some of the most beautiful lush mountains with craggy white peaks I had ever seen. The train arrived in Aguas Calientes at eleven a.m. after the four hour journey. What a surprise upon arrival! The railroad tracks ran right down the middle of the main street in town. I discovered that the railroad was the only way in or out of Aguas Calientes and the whole town was totally pedestrian with the exception of the odd vehicle used to carry goods. Marina, my travel agent, had recommended the Machu Picchu Pueblo Hotel and I was grateful I had booked it in advance.

I saw a man with a white shirt and long black pants holding up a sign with my name on it and I walked over to him and introduced myself. In perfect English he greeted me, reached for my bag, and after a five minute walk we were at the reception desk. The hotel was set in beautiful tropical gardens, large enough to conduct orchid tours and bird watching. The hotel literature at the reception mentioned three hundred and seventy two native orchid species and one hundred and thirty bird species, fourteen of which are hummingbirds that could be found in their gardens. I was warmly greeted and shown to my villa room featuring sliding windows along the wall that completely opened to the lush tropical gardens surrounding the hotel.

After settling into my rustically beautifully suite with locally carved furniture, I decided to get some lunch and scout out the hotel grounds. As I set out on a little exploration mission, I could now see that my hotel sat above the Urubamba River and consisted of red tile-roofed cottages scattered up-slope from the railway station. It was surrounded by its own tropical forest garden with orchid-bedecked trees and boulders. After a walk on the hotel trails in the lush rainforest and discovering numerous butterflies and rare tropical flowers, I circled back to the hotel and found the dining room with its high rustic ceiling, glass walls and outdoor terrace that looked up into the mountain peaks and down into the river chasm below. I resolved to return for dinner, but at the moment I was still interested in checking out more of the town.

I set out down the main street on a walkway that paralleled the railway line down the middle, and I quickly discovered the town's beautiful charm and uniqueness. About five minutes later I found myself in the center of things having passed many shops and restaurants along the way. I had never seen anything like this place. It resembled a town from a Western movie, with frame buildings, covered wooden overhangs and dirt paths. I passed the police station that was a little more modern, made of pale green stucco, with a flat roof and a sign over the door with partially faded let-

24

ters that said, "Comisaria PMP Machupicchu." Oddly, when I looked up I could see a small satellite dish on a rooftop behind, signs of a unique blending of the old quaint Peru and modern technology.

Branching off the main street were other smaller lanes and a main square. Restaurants and shops lined every street, and I chose the first appealing restaurant, Toto's House which was perched over the rapids of the Urubamba River. As I sat there I could look straight up to the mountain top which disappeared into the clouds, the site of the ancient city of Machu Picchu and at the same time, see and hear the rapids of the Urubamba roaring below.

After a great lunch that equaled the best of Cusco, I thought about going up to the top of the mountain to see Machu Picchu but I felt that it was best to make a full day of it, so I resolved to spend the afternoon exploring more of the town sights and fully orient myself to the area. I found a market-lined street that ended at the bus terminus for the trip up the mountain to the sacred city of Machu Picchu, atop the mountain above. During my self-guided tour I found out that Aguas Calientes means hot springs in Spanish. I was then able to locate the natural hot baths, and returned early in the evening for a great soak along with hundreds of other local residents that seemed to use the baths as a regular feature of life here. Machu Picchu and the strange face that I had seen in my inner vision were in my thoughts as I fell asleep that evening.

August 13

The next morning I was up at seven a.m., had an excellent breakfast at the hotel and caught an early bus up to the sacred city. After numerous switchbacks on what seemed like an acrobatic bus, a half an hour later I was at the top and could feel a buzz in my head—a cue to me of the spiritual energy in the location. There lay the city with the steep mountain just behind called Wayna Picchu meaning "young mountain" as opposed to Machu Picchu which means "old mountain." It was truly a stunning vision, the ancient ruins lit in the morning sun with the green spike of Wayna Picchu behind it etched against a clear blue sky.

As I moved forward toward the ruins, something inside drew me toward a wide trail as opposed to what most would do, to explore the ancient site. I could tell it led up to the Inca Trail which was at least five hundred feet above and overlooked the ancient city. So instead I decided to walk up the side of the steep mountain on the trail. Something in me said, "Get a look from up there. Take it all in first." And so I did.

I hiked up the steady incline on the hard-packed dirt path that was imbedded with rocks. Within a half hour I found myself sitting on the edge of a rock outcrop, totally out of breath after the climb at the high altitude, taking in the ancient scene. I later found out that my vantage point was a famous postcard lookout called *The Gate of the Sun* a special place to watch the sunrise over Machu Picchu, and that I had walked up the last section of the ancient Inca Trail, the most tourist traveled section of the trail. The scene was magnificent; the jagged surrounding mountains covered in green scrub foliage looked so verdant, and Machu Picchu was nestled below, now fully illuminated by the morning sun in a hollow between the peaks with Wayna Picchu as a backdrop. It truly was the famous scene that I was taking in.

After surveying the mountain peaks and the ancient city for a few minutes I was ready for my morning Spiritual exercise. I decided to close my eyes and sing HU in this very special place. I wanted to thank Spirit for bringing me this far and for the experience. After what seemed five or so minutes I heard a rock tumble down behind me. I opened my eyes and looked behind. There was another person way up here too? I questioned myself. And then I heard a voice.

In English as clear as a bell I heard, "Would you like some tea?"

I turned around completely, looked up into the sun and stared into a face, the face! The face of the man that I had seen in my contemplation the other morning and also that morning back in St. Louis! He had chiseled features with a broad square forehead and a large flattish nose, and his smile revealed a row of large beautiful white teeth. His skin was golden brown and he was close to my height, about six feet tall, but with a much thicker build. He had wavy, jet black hair combed straight back. And he was wearing a kind of poncho robe of deep burgundy red with royal blue trim. All in all, he appeared to be from a culture I had never seen before.

"Would you like some tea?" he asked again.

I smiled and said, "Who are you?"

He just smiled and said, "Follow me."

I was completely intrigued. He turned and began to move away, and I got up and began to follow. He chose his steps purposefully leading me steeply upward about fifty yards, climbing like a mountain goat. Then he stopped and pointed up.

"Up there," he pointed. As I followed his finger, I could see nestled into the rock-face, what appeared to be a stone hut. It was about another hundred feet up and was blended into the side of the mountain.

"Follow me up there and we will have some tea," he said. I nodded in agreement, trying to catch my breath. I noticed he was very agile and fit and was not out of breath in the slightest. We reached the terrace at what seemed to be the edge of the world and together looked down on the scene of the ancient city.

"Come inside and rest," he said. He held back an animal skin that covered the door, and I moved inside the naturally camouflaged stone hut, looking around at the stone walls and the small fire burning in the center of the room. There was a wooden bunk along one wall and a simple wooden bench along the other. He took up a position on the floor and sat cross-legged in front of the fire. I took off my knapsack and opened my jacket and sat down.

He reached his hand across the short distance between us and smiled a broad smile with his pure white teeth, saying "Thank you for coming and trusting your inner nudges. My name is Chu-Tay, (he pronounced it "Chew-Tay" in two distinct syllables). And of course you are Jack."

"That's right," I said, still trying to take in all that was happening as I reached for his hand. I felt a bit apprehensive, amazed and intrigued at the same time. I thought, here I am in the middle of a stone hut high in the Andes, seventy-two hours and thousands of miles from St. Louis, talking with a man I saw in my spiritual exercises. Chu-Tay could see that I needed some time to settle in with his knowing my name.

"Tea?" he said pointing to the pot sitting over the fire.

I said "sure." I felt more comfortable as he poured out some tea into an old tin cup.

"Do you live here?" I asked.

"Yes, but not all the time. I will explain later. We have not much time. I have something else I need to do in a little while and I want to help you understand how you ended up here."

I was glad to listen and let Chu-Tay do the talking for the moment. He continued: "You have made much progress in your spiritual awareness and it is time for you to take the next step. You have known this in the way you have been feeling lately. Don't you agree?"

I nodded, knowing I had asked Spirit for guidance in being more of service and to help me make my life more purposeful. But this!

"Your coming here to Machu Picchu is no accident," he continued. "You are here in this most ancient and sacred place to find a new purpose in life, and I have come to help you."

I sat in stunned silence listening to his words, spoken with a strong, positive yet kind voice. "We have only two weeks that you have taken for your vacation but I promise you they will be weeks full of spiritual adventure. Are you ready?" he asked.

I smiled and said, "What are you suggesting?"

Chu-Tay replied, "I will help you find your path through your inner awareness. If you agree, we can begin today. Would you like to join me in a spiritual exercise?" I was surprised, but for some reason, at the same time, it seemed completely natural doing a contemplation exercise with him.

"Yes", I said, and we both closed our eyes and began to sing HU. Within seconds I was floating in my consciousness. Then the face of Chu-Tay appeared to me in my inner vision and he began to speak.

" I am going to talk to you about some ancient wisdom to help you make some changes. In this way you can move forward in your wish to serve others and one day you can pass this wisdom on to others. Does this agree with you?"

I inwardly nodded my agreement and Chu-Tay continued to speak:

"There is a set of truths about this life and our world, and I would like to offer you some starting points for you to discover this truth from within your own heart. We all have to find our own truth. It is different for all of us because we all have taken our own path to get here to this present life. We are the sum total of all of our experiences, and our experiences are very unique. And so we are all different and yet we all are the same. We are the same because we have the same origin and are formed of the same substance. This substance is Spirit, a universal "essence". It is everywhere and is the substance out of which everything is formed.

As he spoke I could feel a deep connection with what he was saying.

Our individual essence, a spark of the Divine, is called Soul, and we are a part of this greater "energy" called Spirit, Holy Spirit or the Life Force. Our real existence is as Soul, not our physical body. We are a part of the Creator's creation, and can be considered as a unique part of creation as well as an integral part of the whole. We are actually a Spiritual being that is eternal. As Soul we never die, we unfold.

Chu-Tay continued slowly but deliberately, pausing between his sentences.

As Soul, we have experienced many many lifetimes. Each one has contributed to our inventory of experiences and of course to our growth as this eternal spiritual being called Soul.

Each lifetime is a gift from the Creator that we have earned, an opportunity to learn in a setting that is unique to our spiritual needs. We have complete free will to make decisions and to choose how we react to each action in our day. This is how we learn and how we grow in this lifetime and each other lifetime.

Our lessons from this lifetime, and all others, are recorded in our being as Soul. Our experiences and our reaction to them is what we are, and forms the basis of our lessons today, what is also referred to as karma. We are the best we have ever been in this lifetime and this "best" can be defined as awareness or consciousness, our acceptance of who we are as a part of creation."

Chu-Tay began to fade from my inner vision and said in departing, *"Until tomorrow, then."*

I slowly regained my awareness of the stone floor, the fire and the hut and opened my eyes and looked around. He was gone! I had not heard him leave, but I was alone. I got up, moved to the door and looked out the flap, but no one was there so I moved outside and sat down on the threshold in the bright sunlight. My visions from my Spiritual exercises in St. Louis and in Cusco came back to me. I was looking at the same scene, the mountain peaks, the clear blue sky with the ancient city ruins in the full sun below.

My body reverberated with a chill of recognition.

"Until tomorrow," he had said. And I thought to myself, "What's next?"

Chapter 3
The Journey of Soul

I scaled down the steep mountain slope from the hut to the Inca Trail, often using my hands to grip the rocks to prevent myself from sliding all the way down. I reached the trail in a few minutes, and then I hiked down the mountain from the *Gate of the Sun* toward the well-preserved ruins of Machu Picchu. I was lost in thought about the experience of meeting Chu-Tay and the words that he had spoken to me in our spiritual exercise in the Hut. His final words, "Until tomorrow," rolled over in my mind as I moved along.

I began thinking about my hotel room in Agues Calientes and that it was at least a twenty minute bus ride down into the valley at the foot of Machu Picchu and a ten minute walk to the Machu Picchu Pueblo Hotel. It occurred to me that it would be more convenient if I could stay at the Machu Picchu Sanctuary Lodge right beside the ancient city site, up top, if it was possible. Marina, my travel agent, had said I would need to book the lodge months in advance in order to get a room because of the high demand at the top of the mountain, but I decided to inquire. I got the feeling it was kind of like trying to get a room at the rim of the Grand Canyon in July.

Within a half hour I had trekked down the trail and was at the lodge front desk in the lobby crowded with other tourists. It was twelve thirty p.m. by the time I got there. People were leaving and others were checking in. I waited in line for what seemed to be an eternity and when my turn came, the clerk was polite but firm that there were no rooms available. It would not be as easy to see Chu-Tay tomorrow if there was no room, I thought. The clerk next to mine overheard our conversation and spoke in Spanish to the one serving me. Mine turned to me and said, "This is most rare, Senor, but we have just had a guest check out that is very ill. We will have this room available in about two hours. Would you like it?"

I gratefully accepted the room. With the problem solved, I caught the shuttle bus down to Agues Calientes at the foot of Machu Picchu. The bus headed down the steep switched back road. On each section in the middle we were greeted by a young boy not more than ten years old who was running straight down the fall-line of the mountain, beating the bus at every switch-back level. There must have been sections that were absolutely cliff-like for him to come down, I thought. As the bus passed him he would shout and wave at us. Then he'd take off straight down the mountain to try to beat us to where the road next crossed his vertical trail. Each time he would beat us, and he thoroughly entertained us all the way down to the bottom of the valley at the more than a dozen road and trail crossings. When we arrived at the shuttle bus terminal, he was waiting for us and he jumped on the bus as soon as the driver opened the door to let us off. We all applauded his heroic run down the mountain. He must have made a small fortune in tips for his efforts, since most of the tourists gave him some coins or bills as they got off the bus.

I followed the path from the bus terminus along the train tracks past stalls, shops and restaurants on the main street back to my hotel. I gathered up my few things and toiletries, then checked out of my suite in the Machu Picchu Pueblo Hotel. I walked back through town and caught another bus back up to Machu Picchu. This time I sat on the right side of the bus. After every second hairpin turn switch-back, I could look straight down the side of the valley edge to see the winding switchbacks below and the Urubamba River at the bottom winding along the valley bottom. The bus wheels were no more than a foot or two from the edge of the precipice—and no guard rails! I was hoping we would not pass another bus coming down, but the drivers seemed to have everything well timed to pass where the cliff-hugging road was a little wider!

I dropped off my bag in my new, well-appointed room with extra long twin beds. The hotel was intimate with just thirty-one rooms in the two-story structure. I decided to look around inside to see what the hotel offered in addition to the superb location! The lodge was quite beautiful with colonial architecture and I discovered the cliff-hanging snack-bar that offered a spectacular view overlooking the sacred mountain. There was a formal dining room and an outdoor restaurant that gave lateral views to the ancient site. I was quite hungry, so I sat down outdoors on the patio for lunch and ordered roast chicken, rice and salad.

I spent the later afternoon wandering around the ruins of the ancient city, getting the feel of the place drawn first to what they described as the ancient observatory which was central to the site. I climbed up several sets of stairs to the top and looked out over the entire city. Then I stopped and sat on one of the rocks in the middle and could not help but feel that there had to be more to this than just astronomical observations. I had noticed that the structure was built in layers or steps, like a stepped pyramid. I got up to look over the edge. There were actually numerous steps to the edifice, and I was now more curious about it. I walked down some walkway steps off the top and around to the side of the large structure so that I could see all of the tiers. I began to count the levels; there were fourteen. I knew that was a significant number, but I could not remember where

I had heard the reference. I had been reading many enlightening books in the last few years like the *Conversations with God* series by Neale Donald Walsch, *The Power of Now* by Eckhart Tolle, and several of Harold Klemp's books on Eckankar, but I could not recall the meaning of the number fourteen.

As I continued my exploration of the approximately two hundred buildings that were temples, residences, storage places and other public buildings, I began to notice that the ancient city felt very comfortable. It was like I knew where I was going as I explored the pathways and buildings. I had the strange feeling that I belonged there for some reason. Continuing my discoveries, I noticed the stone walls were well preserved and I was able to walk into many different buildings and get an amazing feel for what it must have been like to have lived there. It actually gave me a little chill as I had the thought. The walls were ceiling height in many. After exploring several of the other ancient buildings, walking up and down numerous steps, I decided to head back to my new hotel just outside the gates of the ruins.

I had a very pleasant dinner in the dining room and then turned in for the night and went to sleep whispering the sound of HU to myself.

August 14

The next morning, I awoke at the crack of dawn, and began my day as usual with my spiritual exercise. It did not take long for Chu-Tay to join me in my contemplation. His smile was beaming as he invited me inwardly to join him for breakfast tea and biscuits up the mountain. I silently agreed and upon completion of my spiritual exercise, showered, shaved and dressed for the climb back up the Inca Trail above the ruins of Machu Picchu and high above the town of Aguas Calientes in the valley below.

The day was crisp, about sixty-five degrees, and the sky was cloudless at almost the top of the mountain. It looked like it would be another perfect day with afternoon highs probably hitting the mid-seventies. We were just thirteen degrees south of the equator, but at such an elevation the weather could not have been more perfect. The valley below was shrouded in mist, still in the shadow of the surrounding mountains. As I climbed past the *Gate of the Sun*, I left the trail and climbed the steep route like a mountain goat up to the hut. I stopped to catch my breath a few times, and each time, I looked down and saw the sunlight gradually illuminate different sections of the ruins below and burn off the occasional wisps of mist in the shaded areas. I chuckled to myself, what a "mist-ical" site. From this distance, I could still clearly make out the stone walls that were in place for most of the buildings about a mile away and about seven or eight hundred feet lower down.

Chu-Tay's voice brought my attention to the climb and the destination. I could see him sitting on the threshold as I made my way closer to his hut, scrambling almost straight up the last part of the ascent. He greeted me with a big smile, the one I had seen an hour before during my contemplation in my room. He had his sleeves rolled up, and I could see that his deep burgundy red robe was not only trimmed in royal blue satin or silk-like material, but that it was lined with this fabric and color as well. He waved me in to the fire and we sat down together, cross legged on the dirt floor. I noticed his leather thongs for the first time. They looked quite worn but solid and appeared hand crafted. The broad straps across the tops of his feet were fur covered with what looked like bristly goat hair. He reached over for the pot and poured some tea for me into the same metal cup as before. He then took the lid off of an old pan and offered me a golden brown, fire-baked biscuit which I accepted.

As I sat back to enjoy the simple breakfast, he began to speak. I noticed how melodious his voice was. It was rhythmical, almost poetic as he spoke. As I finished the flavorful corn-tasting biscuit I could not help but close my eyes and listen to his words:

I spoke last about the eternal nature of Soul. As Soul we exist in a symbiotic relationship with the Creator, in that we are in It and It is in us. By analogy, we are part of the body of God.

As he purposefully spoke, the words seemed to carry me off into a deep contemplation in another dimension.

"Soul exists throughout all time and has had many earthly experiences or incarnations. This journey of Soul, the process of birth, death and rebirth of Soul in the human body is called reincarnation. When people refer to past lives, they are referring to Soul's previous experiences in other incarnations or lifetimes. To make the experiences truly unique and challenging for Soul, our previous incarnations are not given to us as conscious memory in the human body. But as we grow spiritually and gain in our awareness of our true nature as Soul, the memories of our past incarnations that are relevant to our current lessons can be accessed to help us grow from past experiences, many of them that could have been better handled from Soul's spiritual perspective.

At any given point in Its development, Soul can be said to have earned a certain degree of mastery over Itself as an earthbound Spiritual being. This mastery is, in large part, based on the measure of control it has gained over five key negative behaviors or passions of the physical worlds: lust, which is undue craving for things or other people; anger; greed; vanity; and attachment, which means having an undue attachment to things, ideas or persons. As Soul moves through each incarnation or lifetime, It learns and eventually rises above these negative influences on Its behavior, which are part of this schoolhouse of life.

I felt as though I was an observer as well as a participant—like I was listening to him but also watching the two of us from another position nearby as he continued to speak.

Chiefly, however, Soul learns how to give of itself without expecting anything in return. In other words, Soul learns how to love unconditionally. As Soul moves closer and closer to Its goal of learning how to love in greater measure, It becomes more aware of its true nature and begins to operate from a higher viewpoint. Self-realization is defined as this point at which we, while in the physical body, recognize our true self as Soul.

Soul then continues Its eternal journey toward a greater understanding and awareness of its relationship with the Creator. As It becomes more aware of this relationship, It gains in consciousness and, at some point, It is fully aware of its relationship with the Creator or God. This state is often re-

ferred to as God Realization. In reality, Soul is on a journey to become an assistant or co-worker with God here on Earth and in the Spiritual worlds, and to help other Souls. In this journey toward perfection or Spiritual mastery, there is always one more step to be taken. In other words, Soul never stops learning and growing.
Jack, this is the odyssey of Soul.

Chu-Tay's voice trailed off with the words, *"Until Tomorrow."*

His words were still energizing my being as I slowly became aware of where I was and the heat of the fire. I opened my eyes and looked around. As before, I found myself alone to ponder his words. I was still holding the tea cup, and I took a sip of the warm-hot tea, wondering how he was able to slip away without me hearing him. I slowly got up to see if he was outside. I lifted the door covering, stepped out of the doorway and scanned the entire area, but he was nowhere in sight.

I sat on the mountainside next to the hut sipping the tea and surveyed the ancient ruins below with the sun on my face. I was still puzzled about the fourteen tiers that made up the observatory in the middle of the ancient city, so I resolved to spend the day in the city remnants, exploring other areas of the vast site.

Chapter 4
Sound and Light

The next day I was up before the sunrise again. I loved sunrises, something the demands and opportunities of the brokerage business had brought into my life. My spiritual exercise was deeply relaxing as I asked Spirit for guidance for the day. I got a peaceful feeling and also a strong feeling to be alert.

I set out on foot as I had the day before through the sacred city and then up the Inca Trail toward the *Gate of the Sun*. I could see there was someone up ahead, another early riser getting a jump on the crowds. As I wound my way up the trail above the ancient ruins, I could see it was a woman with a small backpack. I stepped up my pace and soon was about 100 feet behind her. I called out, "Good morning," and she stopped and turned around. She was wearing a bright blue silk bomber jacket and a pale green peaked baseball hat and looked to be in her mid-twenties.

I jogged up and stopped. I was immediately exhilarated with her beauty and felt thrill of recognition, like we had met before—but where?

As I beheld her features, my heart felt like it was singing. She had platinum blond hair pulled into a pony tail and clear sparkling blue eyes. She was tall, about five foot eight. Her face and forehead were broad and her blond eyebrows were in perfect arches. She gave me a big smile and said, "Hello" with a strange lilting English accent. I said, "Hello" back.

"Are you trying to catch the sunrise, too?" she asked.

"Yes. I'm meeting a friend up here, too," I replied.
She looked surprised but didn't say anything.

I said, "Let's walk together?" She tilted her head in a slight nod, turned and proceeded up the slope. As I followed watching her pony tail bounce up and down. I could not help but notice how trim she was with slender shoulders, tiny waist and slim hips. She was wearing tight blue jeans with fancy silver stitching on the back pockets and rugged hiking shoes. She appeared quite athletic, moving with strong steady steps.

We walked in silence for the next few minutes, ascending the Inca Trail, as she led the way with me following behind. I was literally stuck for words, a rare occasion for me and I especially didn't want to ask her if we'd met before. It would have sounded like such a bad line. I could not form a thought all the way up to the *Gate of the Sun*, where I needed to leave the trail to ascend toward the hut. When she paused, I pointed up to the ledge a few hundred feet above and said, "My friend is up there," and she turned and looked up.

"Yes," she smiled, "I will continue over to there," as she pointed to an excellent observation point where the sun can be seen to illuminate the ruins one building at a time. I noticed the bright blue and gold crest on her jacket with three crowns in a pyramid shape with the words, "Team Sweden Volleyball" on the top and "Tre Kronor" on the bottom. Somehow I felt that I wanted to get to know her better. Finally a thought came to mind and I asked with a question in my voice, "Maybe we will meet again?"

She smiled broadly, lifted her hat and ran her fingers through her platinum hair, pushing back the long strands to keep them out of her eyes. Then with a slight tilt of her head she turned and made her way over to the point. She was really starting to intrigue me. I surmised to myself *what a coincidence* and then I quickly corrected that thought, knowing that everything in life has significance.

I continued straight up the steep incline off the trail and lost sight of her. I began to think of the big decisions I had made in my life, like leaving law school in the second year, much to the disappointment of my parents. They had great hopes that I would join them in the family practice. Our relationship had been strained for five years as I struggled to find work that had some meaning for me. Eventually I took the securities course and got my license.

And the break- up with Alexis, my high school sweetheart. She too, was upset that I was not going to be a lawyer. She had our life together all planned out. We were going to have two children, vacation at her parent's family estate every August on the coast of Maine, and live in the house of her dreams in a small community just north of St. Louis. She was never the same to me after I left law school, and we gradually drifted apart when her plans for life had to change too. In retrospect, I could see that life with Alexis was going to be her show, and I'm grateful today that I was not caught in her web of materiality. I was searching for a kind of liberty I could not describe in any other way but as a feeling—a sense of freedom without limitations.

The stone hut was now in sight, and as the morning before, Chu-Tay was there, sitting on the threshold watching the sunrise.

"Are you hungry?" he asked.
I said "Not yet."

"Sit down then and we'll watch the sun light up the valley. Listen to the sounds," he said, "All of life is about Light and Sound."

I asked, "What are you doing up here? Are you from here?"

Chu-Tay replied politely, "All in good time Jack, please be patient and all answers will be provided to you.

I nodded my acceptance. As Chu-Tay continued to speak, I was drawn off into another space as I looked down at the sacred city gradually being lit by the sun, one ruin at a time.

"Jack, scientists in recent years have confirmed the fact that there is a basic essence or unit of "energy," at the foundation of everything in the universe. This substance forms the lowest common denominator of everything in creation including Soul. It sustains and is the basis of all life. Some call this The Life Force, Prana, or Holy Spirit as I mentioned to you before. What is important for you to know is that Spirit manifests and can be felt or experienced by human beings as Sound and Light in its two basic forms of vibration."

Chu-Tay paused, and in the silence with just the sound of the morning breeze blowing some grasses nearby, I could hear my usual high-pitched electrical buzzing sound, and then I started to apprehend, very faintly, the sound of crickets—like a field of crickets at night. After a few undetermined moments, I could once again hear the sound of his voice as he continued.

> *"These twin aspects of the universes of vibration, Sound and Light, are actually guideposts for us on our Spiritual journey back to the heart of the Creator. When we begin to see inner Light or hear inner Sounds, we are tuning in to other Spiritual planes or worlds and this can give us the reassurance we need to continue our individual quest for the inner truth we all search for at some point in our existence as Soul. Spiritual Light can manifest in our inner vision as blue light, golden light, white light, of any other color for that matter."*

As he spoke, I thought about the experience I'd had with the blue light.

> *The experiences we can have with Spiritual Sounds are not as well known, but are actually more prevalent once people understand that they are actually hearing a Spiritual Sound and begin to listen for it. The Spiritual Sounds we can hear with our inner hearing differ depending on our state of consciousness at any particular time. They can manifest as the sound of rolling thunder, rushing water, tinkling of bells, buzzing bees, chimes, the single note of a flute, crickets, or a high pitched electronic sound, among others.*

> *Experiences with Light and Sound are spiritual gifts to be treasured."*

Chu-Tay's voice drifted off and I was lost in thought for a few moments thinking about his words and then about my spiritual exercises and how they had changed my life.

46

I was so different now from my law school days ten years ago. I felt so much freer, so content, listening to Spirit each day for my guidance. I was following my heart more and it felt good being here, I thought.

I opened my eyes and Chu-Tay was gone. It still felt like he was there, but he was physically not there. His disappearing like that had really peaked my curiosity though! I sat there looking out at the vista, pondering his message and observing the sun fully lighting the valley and the ancient city way below. It seemed to be a metaphor for Chu-Tay's messages for me—illuminating certain new ideas for me as well. My thoughts immediately shifted to the woman I had met on the way to the hut. I resolved to see if she was still on the vantage point she had selected for the sunrise. I scaled down the rock slope to the trail and walked out to the point where she had headed but she was gone. I wasn't doing well this morning—two people disappearing on me, I chuckled to myself.

I decided to head down and do some more exploring in the ruins. From my high vantage-point I could now see they were actually situated in an enclave on the saddle of the mountain that overlooked the deep canyon of the Urubamba River and the lush tropical forest of the valley floor below.

Who knows, I thought, maybe I will see her there?

Chapter 5
The Meaning of Life

The literature in my hotel room said that Machu Picchu was discovered by American explorer Hiram Bingham in 1911, and is considered to be one of the most extraordinary examples of landscape architecture in the world. In scanning the brochure earlier, I had also discovered that Machu Picchu served as a place of worship, as well as a site for star-gazing. In addition, it was a private hacienda of the family of the Inca Pachacutec. I strolled around the two main sections, and could see for myself that one was the agricultural area which consisted mainly of terraces, mountain slopes and food stores. Then I found myself in the main ruins that archeologists consider the urban area, which is noted for its sacred buildings, temples, squares and royal tombs. I could see it had been built with a high degree of skill. I followed the many stairways and canals carved out of stone around the site for another couple of hours, looking in many of the buildings.

Most of the structures were built of granite blocks that were smoothed and that none of the blocks were the same size. The joints were incredibly tight and in many places the architecture was blended into the landscape, as existing stone formations were used in the construction of many structures. Sculptures were carved into the rock in many places. Houses seemed to be built in groupings around communal courtyards or were aligned on slender terraces, connected by narrow alleys. At the center were the open squares and livestock enclosures.

I decided to climb back up to the top of what they called the observatory for another look at the whole scene. In the back of my mind, I was keeping an eye out for the woman in the bright blue silk jacket. I sat on a large stone block in the middle, and then I changed to face each of the other directions in turn. By this time I was beginning to feel the presence of tour groups, and I wanted to find a quiet spot and sit in the early afternoon sun. I looked around and could see on the edge of the site on the main section below, a wall that I could sit on that was on a slope, away from where the tour groups were led.

After a ten minute walk over to my secluded spot, I sat down and relaxed. I could look down over the nearby ancient walls still standing on terraces that were planted with maize when the city was a thriving center. Closing my eyes and out of habit, I started to sing HU with the faint sound of voices and the gentle breeze in my ears. The sound reverberated in my head as I felt myself lift in consciousness. After a few minutes, I began to see a picture forming. In a moment I was back in the hut and Chu-Tay was sitting cross-legged on the floor across from me. He smiled and said, "Welcome back." I could sense that we were not alone but I could only see Chu-Tay. He began to speak and I sat in quiet contemplation now enjoying the experience.

"There are some golden keys that I would like to offer to help you understand the true meaning of life. As I have said to you before, as Soul we incarnate into a body at birth. Our body is worn like a covering for Soul and allows us to work through our lifetime of experiences needed for Soul's purification and ascent into the higher worlds of God.

Our growth is a process of trial and error but there are really no errors, just growth and unfoldment for Soul. Just like the movie-making process is a series of "miss-takes" until you get a" take" so our life is a process of experiences from which we learn. There is no failure, only missed opportunities for Soul's growth. There is always one more opportunity, as there is always one more step in the unfoldment of Soul. Lessons are repeated until they are learned. In fact, lessons keep returning as we reach higher and higher levels of understanding regarding certain issues that Soul has chosen to focus on. Every part and action of life contains an experience for Soul's growth.

As he spoke, I noticed my inner vision was bathed in a soft yellow light.

As we begin to understand that life is more than a series of destinations, we start to slow down and put more attention on the journey. The process of traveling to our endless destinations is as important as achieving the goals we create for ourselves throughout life. This realization is a major step in our awakening. It is the realization that how we create our lives and the methods we use, is really how Soul grows and, therefore, what is of ultimate importance. The journey is really what life is all about. Material goals are simply tools for Soul's growth.

The help we need for all of life's difficulties is right inside us. In other words, all the answers to all of our challenges are given to us if we ask. It is up to us to seek these answers, and to use our creativity to draw them out. The process is a challenging one but rewarding for Soul. Knowing that all the answers are within allows us to take a gentle ap-

proach to life. It allows us to walk in confidence knowing that all we have to do is listen for the inner nudges, or feel the heart to "hear" the call of Soul.

As we live our lives, we are awakening to new levels of awareness of who we truly are and why we are here, and this is a never ending process of discovery. There is always one more step in Soul's growth.

This is enough for now. I will give you more details later.

The scene began to fade, but not before I caught a glimpse in my inner vision of another being in the hut and a flash of blue. It was her—the beautiful woman from the morning ascent up the mountain! Some chatter about thirty feet away brought me abruptly back to my physical awareness, and I opened my eyes to see what was happening. A group of Japanese tourists were being led through the ruins, and the guide was pointing out the archaeological features in their language.

After such an interesting morning and afternoon, I decided to head back to the lodge for the evening, still wondering whether I had really seen the woman in my spiritual exercise or whether it had been my wishful thinking. On the way back I thought about some of the things Chu-Tay had said about life being like a movie, a series of "miss-takes" and the other changes I had made in the preceding years. I had quit smoking three years ago, a very difficult challenge in the brokerage business where practically everyone it seemed, smoked in our office. The mistake was even starting in the first place. I hadn't bought my first pack until after leaving law school and I guess that along with the transition to finding my new groove in life was all about being a rebel. I also thought it would help me keep the weight off. But the half a pack a day turned into two packs a day, and I began to feel that it could eventually affect my voice. The cough that wouldn't go away was the trigger to dump the habit.

And partying in the bars every week became a drag as well. Beer never tasted the same without cigarettes, and I also became very sensitive to smoke. Lots of changes in the last three years, I thought, but worth it. I could climb up to the hut without even running out of breath now and at this altitude as well! Not bad for thirty-three years of age.

The sun dipped below the mountain peaks as I entered the Machu Picchu Sanctuary Lodge for the evening. My thoughts drifted to the experience of meeting the beautiful woman and seeing her in my contemplation. I was now sure the experience was real.

Chapter 6
The Creative Power of Soul

As I lay in bed after dinner I was still thinking about the woman and still flip-flopping over in my mind whether I had seen her in my afternoon contemplation at the ruins, or not. Not only was she beautiful, there was something about her that really intrigued me, and I felt attracted to her in a way I have never felt before with any of the many women I had gone out with. Even with Alexis, when we first met, I had been physically attracted to her, but I did not have this strange excited sensation I now felt for the woman in the bright blue silk jacket. There was something about her voice: It was sweet sounding, and so kind, yet there was a communication of confidence as she spoke as well. I really wanted to see her again and talk to her. My thoughts then drifted to the things Chu-Tay had said, like our true reality being Soul, his message about growth being a process of trial and error, and learning lessons in every lifetime. With these thoughts rolling over in my mind, I fell asleep.

<u>August 16</u>

I awoke at my usual hour before dawn, showered and dressed for the day. I then sat down to do my morning spiritual exercise and decided to ask some questions in contemplation. I began with singing HU several times, and then I got a nudge to shift to the new mantra sound that had come to me a while ago, the sound "Mahanta". I began to sing "Mahanta" in a slow drawn out way like "Maah-haantaah", and the inner sound began to come as the sweet sound of violins playing in the distance. The gentle resonance was absolutely beautiful. Then the light that I was looking for with gentle expectation began to appear in my inner vision, electric blue, just like the time that I was shoveling snow at my dad's house. It was vibrant with a golden corona and all I could do was to go with the experience and watch and listen. It began to fade after about a minute, and I was conscious of still gently singing Ma-han-ta.

I asked inwardly, "What does Mahanta mean?"

For a moment there was silence, and then I sensed the presence of Chu-Tay and the subtle thought impression, *Master of Masters.*

As I slowly came back to physical consciousness, I had the strong feeling my questions would be answered that day about the attractive woman and Chu-Tay. I reached for my journal and made a note of having this special blue light experience and hearing distant violins. Then I took another few minutes to add some thoughts about what had transpired yesterday.

I left the hotel room earlier than before and hung around outside hoping to get a glimpse of the woman in case she was going to repeat her trip up the mountain to see the sunrise, but after ten minutes I decided I had better get on my way. Just as the sunlight was breaking on the mountain top, I could see the hut, but Chu-Tay was not in sight yet. I continued climbing. As I approached the entrance, I could hear voices inside, and then I heard Chu-Tay say, "Come in Jack."

I pulled back the flap, and there sitting on the floor, to my utter amazement, was the woman! She was wearing the same mid-blue silk jacket and light green hat, but her long blond hair was down and covered her shoulders. She and Chu-Tay were sitting cross-legged on the hard-packed dirt floor sipping tea.

Chu-Tay said, "Jack this is Lena. We have been expecting you."

She smiled a big, genuinely natural smile.

I reached out my hand and said, "Hello again, I'm Jack." How did you get here?" She took my hand and we shook for a moment, and I could not help noticing the softness, yet strength, of her grip. Touching her stirred something in me beyond explanation.

Chu-Tay raised his hand and said, "All in good time Jack. You and Lena have much in common. Please be patient. I would like to talk to you both today about some things the two of you have been asking about in your contemplations."

I was totally baffled, but I was getting used to surprises these days, so I chilled and tried to remain calm and cool in Lena's presence. I got myself comfortable on the floor and began sipping the tea Chu-Tay had already poured for me before I arrived.

As Chu-Tay spoke, I could see Lena's eyes slowly close and I found it easier to do the same, although I could not help looking at her for a moment or two. I realized my heart was beating like a drum, and it took me a minute to settle down after meeting her again!

"The two of you are starting to create new lives. This can be aided by using the creative power of Soul. This creative power is inherent in all of us,

yet lies largely dormant in most. You are actually taught in your society to favor the mental process as there is very little attention given to inner creativity and its development as you grow up and through your schooling in Western society.

However, the two of you are ready to take the next step. The process involves an understanding that one must work at any skill to become good at it. Our creative power is no different. It requires attention and the more attention we give it, the more easily our creativity can flow."

What are the benefits of developing creative power? I asked inwardly.

"For most, it means to operate from a different viewpoint, a higher viewpoint—that of Soul. This viewpoint has numerous advantages such as being able to see life from a greater sense of vision or perspective. In a practical sense, this offers one solutions to life's challenges. Developing your creative power can lead to a greater attunement with your inner self and your true desires, your heart. In addition, tuning in to hunches along with developing a greater trust in following your nudges and intuition are benefits. The development of this creative power can also include bringing clarity to your dreams, and give you the ability to see and interpret waking dreams—signs from God- when life's circumstances seem to be guiding one."

How can I develop my creative power? I thought. Chu-Tay continued.....

"There is one specific activity that is important to developing the creative power of Soul and there is another that you can begin to focus upon to help you transition to creating your own life. The first is to maintain your contemplative or spiritual exercises every day. Just like a physical exercise, doing this will activate your spiritual "muscle". You need to give yourself about 15 or 20 minutes of your time each day, at the same time each day if possible. Doing this, you will shift from "thinking" your way through life to "feeling" or "sensing" your way through life. Life was meant to flow for us, and this is one way to begin to really go with the flow.

The other action is to slow down. In today's world most people are running through life. They are so busy they can hardly catch their breath or the inner nudges that Soul is offering."

Chu-Tay's, voice began to fade as he concluded, *"You can start by taking just one thing out of your day to begin to allow more time. Also, try to walk slower as you go about your day.*

I'll provide further guidance in the days to come."

I slowly began to open my eyes and gained my physical awareness. There was something in the sound of his voice that seemed to take me to another level of consciousness, each time he spoke. Lena was just opening her eyes as well. We looked at each other, looked around, and found we were alone. I had so many questions, I didn't know where to start.

"That was amazing! How did you find Chu-Tay?" I asked.

"In my contemplations." she replied with that sweet lilting accent I had heard yesterday.

"How did you find him?" she asked as she slowly began to rise.

"The same way as you." I said as I got up.

I followed her out of the hut. "Would you like to talk?" I asked half knowing the answer.

She replied, "I want to be alone just now to think about what he has said. How about later, perhaps at dinner?

"That would be great," I responded, trying not to sound too excited. "How about six in the dining room?"

She smiled, revealing a row of perfect white teeth and replied, "That will be wonderful."

Excellent, I thought to myself, she said "wonderful". She appeared at some times to be coy, and yet she was so direct as well. She was really different.

She cocked her head a little and turned and headed down the steep incline to the trail. I followed her down the steep slope and then quietly along and down the trail in a kind of walking contemplation. I wanted to speak with her more, but I knew we both had a lot to process from Chu-Tay's message in the hut. When we reached the bottom of the trail, about fifty yards from the ruins of the lost city, she turned, pleasantly smiled and said, "Jack, I will see you in the lodge dining room at six o'clock."

I replied with enthusiasm, "Excellent. Where are you from?"

She answered, "I'm Swedish. See ya at six then," and then she leaned over to my complete surprise and gave me a gentle kiss on the cheek, then immediately turned and headed in the direction of the ruins. No other woman had ever done that to me! My heart was truly singing, and I could not wait to see her at dinner. I would have to do something for the rest of the day to keep my sanity, I thought.

After her kiss and feeling her hair brush against my face, I found myself staring at the mountain that sits behind Machu Picchu. It dawned on me that this mountain called Wayna Picchu would be a great vantage point to observe the ancient ruins, and I had read that there was a trail up to the top. I walked back down to the lodge and up to the reception desk.

"Would you have some information on the trail up Wayna Picchu?" I asked.

The girl smiled, reached down and pulled out a document, unfolding it as she spread it out on the counter. I sensed that this was a common question they were asked. When she got it unfolded, I could see that it was a map of the Inca Trail and other trails in the area. With marker in hand, she drew on the map showing me the direction leaving the lodge, handed me the map with a smile and advised, "Wayna Picchu is a good climb, but be sure to start down before three o'clock because it can get dangerous when the light gets too low on the other side. There are some very steep sections, but there are ropes along the trail in some areas to help trekkers up these places."

I thanked her for the map and the climbing tips and then asked her if she could book Lena and I into the dining room at six o'clock, as it was not open yet for reservations.

She said she would take care of it. I then walked down the hall to the cafeteria and had a big breakfast of eggs, toast, bacon and coffee, watching the sun come up and illuminate the entire high-altitude saddle-shaped valley. There were a few clouds and it looked like a perfect day for a climb.

I went back to my room and grabbed my day-pack, then dropped back by the cafeteria and got a large bottle of water and a few energy bars out of two vending machines. As I headed out of the hotel it was about eleven o'clock. I felt glad this climb would be a challenge. I really needed something to take my mind off Lena and the anticipation I was feeling about meeting her for dinner. I was now hearing the sound of her voice as music in my head and heart.

I reached the trailhead at Wayna Picchu after an hour's hike over some up and down terrain that formed a thin ridge. It stretched from the ancient city to the "young mountain." I realized I was actually climbing only the top quarter of the mountain, the part that rose above and behind Machu Picchu, the "old mountain." The climb turned out to be more challenging than running the rapids on the Colorado when I was white water rafting a couple of years ago.

The trail started out winding steeply upward and consisted of hard packed dirt with many rocks imbedded that were good for footholds. The vegetation was scrub-like with grasses and bushes. As I proceeded, I came upon sections that were very steep with rocks that had been used to make a rough staircase ascending sharply. The trail and stairs seemed very old, and I could see that most steps were worn down a few inches, indicating that many had climbed this mountain for hundreds or perhaps even thousands of years before. Then I came upon a section where the stairs were steeper than the angle that you would place a ladder against a wall, and I thought, "How am I going to get down this if I get up there?

I looked around, and then I saw the rope. I was glad the receptionist had mentioned it as it gave me the confidence to keep going, knowing that many others had made it. It was thick and knotted and appeared to be anchored at the top. I could see it was also tied at the bottom around a rock, so I pulled hard on it and it held firm. Dragging the rope over to the edge of the staircase, I looped my arm around it as I climbed up the stairs using my hands and feet. I thought the easiest way to descend might be to kind of rappel down or go hand-over-hand down the rope.

I made it to the top of the almost vertical stepped section. The path followed a ledge for a while, and I was able to catch my breath and get my strength back. There was a lot of foliage along the narrow trail, and I began to notice that I could hear rushing water like a waterfall up ahead. A little further along, as I edged around a corner, I came upon the falling water and a big surprise. The area was thick with foliage, like a jungle. It was like a whole other ecosystem had been created by the micro-climate of the falling water. The stream was cascading down, creating a mist that watered the foliage. There were several orchids and other unknown flower varieties peeking out from the tangled vines and branches which were blocking the trail and I wondered how I was going to get through.

As I stood there and looked around, I gazed out over the edge of the cliff into the abyss. There was no way going down, so I turned and surveyed the rock face. I noticed foot-holds about four inches deep, carved into the rock wall which led up at a sharp angle. As I studied the wall,

I could see that there were also natural rock hand-holds I could easily reach. It wasn't as bad as I thought, so I carefully put my foot into the first hole and grabbed the natural handgrip above my head that was worn smooth over the years. Soon I was gripping with all fours going up the face, observing where the foot-holds and hand-grips were for each move up. I had only done rock climbing once on a man-made wall during a visit to California, and now those memories were giving me the confidence I needed to proceed. After three or four minutes I came to another ledge about four feet wide about twenty feet up from where I had started. I had made it!

I sat on the edge of the ledge looking out over the valley and almost straight across to Machu Picchu, although I was a little higher. I was able to see more clearly the original agricultural terraces and ruins of the storehouses in the high altitude valleys surrounding the old city. After a few minutes, I continued my climb and followed the trail as it wound its way, circling around the other side of the mountain, moving steadily upwards. The rest of the climb was relatively easy and uneventful, following the cliff-like edge of the mountain, although some sections got as narrow as two feet. I had to inch my way along facing the rock wall since my pack stuck out too far to do it facing outward. I enjoyed the perfect air temperatures, the sunshine and the gentle wind.

An hour and a half from the starting point, I reached the trail summit and sat down for a rest. I opened my pack and ate some of my snacks as I looked out over the valleys. I could see down in one direction to the Urubamba River in the distance and my eye followed it, meandering east through more mountains where it disappeared from view. I thought about it winding its way into the Peruvian tropical rainforests to the east, and then into Brazil where it would connect with the Amazon River. I mused that that would be the mother of all rafting trips, all the way to the Atlantic from the high Andes! Then my thoughts drifted to a recollection of some of the words Chu-Tay had spoken about our creative power. He had said, "It involves the development of a greater attunement with our inner self and our true desires," and I realized that my true desire was to get to know Lena better. As I sat there thinking about my inner self, I realized there was something about her energy and her voice that stirred my heart.

It was pushing two o'clock in the afternoon, and I decided to head back down to the hotel before I thought too much about some of the sections I would have to climb down. I wanted to have plenty of time to rest up before dinner, and I did not want to be late!

The descent was actually not as challenging because it was easier on the lungs. I just had to stay very focused. The big challenge turned out not to be the stairs with the rope. The vertical section beside the waterfall was the toughest part because I couldn't see the footholds as I stepped backwards over the edge. I had to feel around for each one with my foot to find them. Once I got the hang of that, I was able to make my way down, but the wall and hand grips were wet and slippery. The breeze had shifted, and the mist from the waterfall was getting me quite wet. I decided I needed to be very patient and just take my time and not be in a rush, reminding me of Chu-Tay's words earlier about slowing down and feeling my way through life.

The rest of the trail was uneventful but, I thought, as I hiked down the last rough stone staircase, I can chalk this climb up as one of the most challenging adventures in my life. Little did I know what was to come. But I had definitely accomplished my mission; taking my mind somewhat off the dinner date with Lena.

Chapter 7
Reincarnation

Back in my room I flopped down on the bed and rested for an hour or so, then showered and got out the best clothes I had brought. I put on my black casuals and my favorite light blue denim shirt. I was ahead of schedule so I decided to go downstairs to the dining room a little early. I was excited and wanted to make sure the table was ready. I waited in line for two other parties to be seated, then the hostess greeted me with a courteous "buenos noches." and checked me off her list. I followed her across the busy room to a table beside the front window and she removed the little American Express reserved sign as she left. I felt like I could have been in any restaurant around the globe except for the fact that I was looking out on one of the wonders of the world.

From my seat I could also keep an eye on the entrance. I scanned the room to make sure she wasn't already there, as a waiter came to fill my water glass. I wouldn't want to make that mistake, sitting there waiting for her while she was waiting for me. But I was sure she was not there yet. I looked out the window at the ancient city, bathed in evening light. After mulling over events all afternoon, I had so many questions.

I felt someone at the table. I looked up, and there she was with her hand outstretched for mine. With a big, beautiful smile she took my hand gently but confidently, and said, "Hello Jack," in that lilting accent of hers. I began to get up, but she sat down before I could rise and continued, " I'm so sorry for not talking to you after our meeting with Chu-Tay this morning. It was rude of me, but I did need to have some space. I needed to think about things."

"I needed to have some time, myself," I responded, knowing that if I'd had a choice, I would have stayed and talked with her that morning. She was wearing tight black leather pants and a red silk blouse. I saw that more than one head turn to look at her when she arrived. She had changed her hair, and it was now long and flowing with waves along her cheeks, the rest combed up high over her forehead then falling down to her shoulders. Her lips were vibrant red, matching her blouse, and her eyes looked even more blue than I remembered this morning. She was positively stunning!

I was bubbling inside as I asked her about her day. "What did you do today? Did you have any more inner experiences?"

"No, she reflected, "I went down to Agues Calientes below and got lost in the markets and stalls for several hours. I really wanted to take my mind off things and it really worked. Things were happening too fast for me."

She looked straight into my eyes as she said the last sentence. I felt she was talking about meeting me, but I could not be sure. She leaned closer putting her arms on the table and asked, "What did you do today, Jack?"

"I found a way to take my mind off things like you did, but it turned out to be a lot more than I expected!" I told her about my climb and the section beside the waterfall, and I could see a slight look of concern in her eye, as though she could be concerned for my safety. As we talked, there was something about her that excited me, but it was not just her beauty. I felt a comfort with her as well.

Our conversation soon drifted from our day's adventures to our spiritual experiences. I asked her about Chu-Tay and she told me that she, too, had discovered contemplation from a former boyfriend, a pilot, about three years ago. Chu-Tay had appeared to her in her inner experiences in much the same way it had happened for me. Our conversation then drifted naturally into our present circumstances and how our lives had brought us to this point. She told me she was a model in Sweden in her earlier days and was now a magazine fashion consultant in Chicago. I thought to myself, *that's only about four hours drive from St. Louis.* From what I was able to piece together later, I figured her to be in her early thirties. She had a look about her that was so fresh, so full of natural energy, I felt she could easily pass for mid-twenties, as I had originally thought.

I told her about my last ten years, leaving law school, the split up with Alexis and becoming a stock broker, as well as other changes I'd made in the last few years. She was completely in sync with what I was saying. She had been a party girl in the modeling profession, drinking and smoking and attending late night parties all over the world. But she had come to a point where it was no longer how she wanted to feel. She discovered it was a hollow life in the end, and she was ready to move on. I asked about her bright blue team jacket and found out that she loved volleyball and that her team, Tre Kronor, the same lettering as on her jacket crest, meant "Three Crowns." She said that she played for Sweden at the Olympic Games and that she still plays for fun in Chicago in a local league. No wonder she was in such good shape, I thought. She confided, "volley-ball was my continuity in life when I was doing all that party-ing. It kept me grounded and gave me a sense of purpose."

My heart was sensing the synchronicity. It seemed as though we had come through similar events and led paral-lel lives from a spiritual growth perspective. We both real-ized life could offer more than just an endless cycle of fun and self-gratification. It was truly amazing how much we shared with each other after just meeting, how open we were with each other, talking about our past and how we were both able to see our lives from the same perspective. I had never before experienced a first "date" where I shared so much with a lady and we felt so comfortable with each other. It almost seemed like there were no barriers to our communication and that I could talk about anything with her. And there was so much more I wanted to know about her life and her parents and the rest of her family. Later I re-flected that perhaps it had something to do with having the experience together with Chu-Tay.

We were having coffee when we came back to dis-cussing our experiences with spirituality, contemplations, and the HU. She had started to do contemplations three years ago, after she had changed jobs and given up smok-ing and alcohol. It turned out she did her contemplations just before bed, whereas I like to do mine in the morning. We talked about our contemplation with Chu-Tay that morn-ing. Then she surprised me, as we both finished our coffee at the same time.

"Would you like to do a contemplation together?" she asked. "We could go up to my room." I was stunned with her forward approach, but we had shared so much in the last hour and a half that I was more than ready to agree, especially since I'd wanted to see her all day.

"That would be great. It will be very interesting to be together in the inner worlds and maybe we can both see Chu-Tay?" I offered. I had never done a contemplation with anyone else before, so this was a new adventure for me.

I helped her out of her chair, leaving more than enough money on the table to cover the bill that had yet to be presented. She looped her arm into mine as we left the dining room. We took the stairs one flight up and walked down the hall, and she slipped her arm out from mine and found her key, opened the door and turned on a table light. I could see that her room was the same as mine, with one chair and desk, a dresser and twin beds. Several of her outfits were laid out on the bed as if she had been trying on different clothes before coming down for dinner. To me, I thought, anything she wore would have looked great on her. She sat down on the floor at the end of one of the beds with her back resting on the end and positioned herself on the floor cross-legged. I knew I could not sit that way for very long without getting cramps in my legs, so I moved across the room and sat in the chair, my usual position for my contemplations.

She looked over at me with a loving look to see if I was ready and then looked forward and closed her eyes. She began to sing HU and I joined her after a deep breath to relax myself, to try and calm the flutter in my heart. After about ten HU's I began to hear my inner sound and then started to see a familiar face form in my inner vision. Chu-Tay was beaming a bright smile as he said hello to both of us. But I could not see Lena as Chu-Tay continued:

*"I would like to talk to the two of you about the od-
yssey of Soul and shed some light on the meaning
of reincarnation. Reincarnation has nothing to do*

with our physical body and everything to do with our true identity as Soul. We were created and exist because the Creator loves us. Soul's main goal is to learn how to love the way God loves Soul.

This lifetime is a precious gift although it may not seem so to most of us during difficult times. Yet these difficult times are exactly why we are here and serve Soul's growth the most. In other words we grow the most in these difficult life challenges. Our choices are at our complete discretion and we have complete freedom to choose our actions, thoughts and words. It is these reactions that make up our lifetime of experiences.

In every lifetime we have been given a custom tailored set of circumstances to encounter and these are set up as a result of our previous reactions to life in other lifetimes as Soul. These responses to previous challenges are recorded in our Causal Body, part of Soul's make-up. These "records" and the urge we have to revisit lessons is called karma. Our Causal Body, this energy about us "magnetizes" us to certain circumstances. It draws us or attracts us to people and situations in varying degrees, based on the degree of the lesson that must be worked out. We are given yet another opportunity to experience the same challenge and to select a response from a higher viewpoint. I think you will agree that you two are feeling an attraction to each other, like you have been magnetized to one another.

As Chu-Tay spoke I felt an incredible lightness, like I was floating above my chair, unable to feel my arms or legs.

Soul has had literally thousands of lifetimes of experience in this world and in others. These experiences are referred to as incarnations. In our various incarnations we have had the opportunity to exist in every possible social position from King and Queen to peasant and slave. We have "lived" in every part of this world and others, and have experienced being every race and being male and female. We have been martyrs and we have killed others willfully and in war. But one thing is certain, and that is we are the best we have ever been in this lifetime. This means that we are the highest consciousness that we as Soul have ever achieved.

And so reincarnation is the odyssey of Soul. It is how Soul learns. It is Soul's movement through its existence growing at its own pace and in its own time and in its own unique way."

With these last words, Chu-Tay's voice faded, and I became conscious of my body and of the weight of it in the chair. I slowly moved a finger and then stretched my neck and back and opened my eyes. Lena was just coming back as well, and we looked at each other. I could see that she was thinking the same thing I was, that we were attracted to each other in a very strong way that was hard to explain in words. Chu-Tay had confirmed this with us both. But what did it mean?

I said in a quiet voice, "Did you hear that?' and she nodded in agreement. After a moment or two, I began to rise slowly and she did the same. I moved to the door, and she turned to face me and looking at me almost eye to eye, deeply into my eyes. Then she gave me a light kiss on the cheek, lightly brushing my lips with her hair. I returned her affection and gave her a kiss on her cheek. I was going to hug her, but she was not responding, so I quickly moved back a little. I definitely did not want to push the agenda and ruin a good beginning. Better leave it in her hands, I thought. I recovered and asked, "Would you like to walk together to the hut tomorrow morning?

"Yes, that would be lovely," she smiled, "let's meet in the lobby at five-thirty."

"Excellent," I replied as I reached for the door handle.

"Goodnight, Jack," she said with a melody in her voice.
On the way to my room, my heart and stomach was feeling like I was on a roller-coaster, a profound feeling of being exhilarated.
Back in my room I thought about all the things she had told me about her life and how we'd led amazingly parallel lives. And then I thought about Chu-Tay's words, "You two are feeling an attraction to each other like you have been magnetized to one another." I wondered about this and about the deeper meaning of my attraction to her, the first time I had thought about this with any woman. My exhilarated feeling returned and I asked inwardly what this meant.
The word "love" entered my consciousness. Could I be in love with Lena?

I drifted off to sleep thinking about the kiss she had given me and her scent, the scent of fresh wild flowers.

Chapter 8
The Spiritual Worlds

August 17

 I was up at five a.m., quickly showered and shaved, and sat down to do my contemplation spiritual exercise for the day. I got the nudge to begin with the new word I had been trying, "Mahanta". As I began to quietly sing and fill my heart with love, I could feel myself lifting and getting lighter as I sang "Mahantaaaaaaa" in a long drawn out way for the fifth time. I began to look for spiritual light and listen for the inner sounds. I heard a high pitched electrical sound which began to get a little louder, and then I began to see a brightness in my peripheral vision, even though my eyes were closed. It got brighter and brighter until I felt like I was in the dark with bright lights around me. I could feel the presence of Chu-Tay and love, and then I had a strong feeling of Lena. I could almost smell her wildflower scent. There was an unexplainably deep attraction growing in me that was beyond her physical beauty. I wanted just to be with her, to be in her presence, a feeling I had never experienced before.

 My contemplation was positively enlivening as I felt bathed in the sound and golden bright light that came into my inner vision. Then the light faded first, followed by the sound, and I came back to physical consciousness. I opened my eyes, and looked at my watch. It was five twenty-five. I put on my jacket and headed downstairs. Lena was there and greeted me with a big smile.

"How did you sleep?" I asked.

"I had an amazing dream," she said with excitement. "Let's go, and I will tell you on the way."

She slipped her arm through mine which gave me an inner thrill, and we set out on the Inca Trail up the mountain slope. On the way she began to describe the dream. "I was in a small hut with just one window, and I couldn't leave. I was very unhappy and cried for a long while. Then you came and took my hand and led me away, running through the forest. We ran and ran until we were exhausted. We were being followed, and so we had to keep going. And then the dream ended."

I thought about her dream and about what Chu-Tay had said, that we had much in common. But nothing came to mind about the meaning of her dream.

"Perhaps it was a past life experience," I speculated, but she did not pick up my feeling on this and continued in silence, pondering the meaning of her dream. As the trail narrowed, she slipped her arm out from mine, and I dropped back to follow her. We passed by the *Gate of the Sun*, left the trail and headed up the rocky incline to the hut. We were just reaching the ledge when Chu-Tay greeted us as he emerged from the doorway. "Come, let's walk a while," he said as he motioned with his arm sweeping to the right. Chu-Tay led us along the ledge over to a ridge in the early morning light where we could see down the entire length of the valley. He invited us to sit and watch the sun illuminate all of the ruins and the valley below.

As we sat, Chu-Tay began to speak with that strangely melodious and captivating voice of his.

"As Soul, we dwell in spiritual worlds or planes as they are often called, very real places that exist at other vibrations."

Soon my eyes were closed as he spoke to the two of us.

"Science is just beginning to discover the existence of these spiritual realms that vibrate at rates outside our human perception. Many people are sensitive to the world immediately adjacent to the physical plane called the Astral Plane. This plane corresponds to our own astral body that we each carry. Soul maintains a body that corresponds to each plane.

As he spoke, I thought I could hear the sound of the ocean. It can't be, I thought,...it must be the wind.

"The astral plane and the corresponding body are the seat of our emotions. When we are at the astral consciousness we are learning to master our emotions, rather than letting our emotions rule us. We are better able to select our responses as opposed to simply reacting in an 'emotional' manner.

The next plane is the Causal. For this, we also have a corresponding body. The causal plane is the area where the records of all of our past experiences are kept. We can actually access these records if it is in our best interest. It is often useful to understand what is behind a fear, a challenge or a habit that is giving us difficulties in our life. If the root cause is a past life experience, we can be shown this and through the conscious awareness of the cause and acceptance of responsibility for it, we can begin to move past the problem in our life."

For a brief moment, I thought I perceived distant tinkling bells.

The Mental Plane is next and is the seat of the mind. When we are learning about our true nature as Soul and we are working at this level of consciousness, we are learning how to use the mind as a tool and to work from the higher viewpoint of Soul. Specifically, we are learning how to use the creative power of Soul and to operate with the heart, the gut and the mind.

The sound of running water drifted upon my hearing as he continued.

The top of the Mental Plane is called the Etheric Plane and is a place of transition for Soul, the consciousness where we are preparing to operate from the viewpoint of Soul predominantly. In this space, we are redefining ourselves and our values and repositioning ourselves for a life of service, a total reversal from the typical life in the lower worlds that is focused on serving the self.

The sound of running water now became the sound of buzzing bees, growing stronger and stronger as I followed his richly cadenced voice.

So we first learn to gain a fair degree of mastery over our emotions, and when we have reached a great measure of emotional balance, we move on to focus on our past life influences and begin to resolve the lessons we set in motion in previous lives. We are in the causal consciousness at this stage of our spiritual growth. We then progress to the mental consciousness where we learn that thought and intelligence need to be balanced with intuition and listening to the whisperings of Soul. In this state we are beginning to feel as opposed to thinking our way through life and its challenges, working from the viewpoint of Soul.

The etheric consciousness is the transition stage to working as Soul as our primary way of being.

The sound of the buzzing bees in my inner hearing began to diminish and in its place I could hear the faint sound of a flute emerge. I followed the intriguing melody as he continued to speak.

Upon reaching the Soul Plane, a state of conscious awareness, we have realized who we really are; Spiritual Beings. Some call this Self-Realization. Following many higher stages of development as Soul including an interim step, Spiritual Realization, we gain a true awareness of the Creator or God. This awareness is called God Realization.

These are the lower spiritual worlds, the first planes we inhabit on our journey as Soul. Essentially, Soul learns how to love and then how to share this love with all life. We are all walking this path at our own pace in our own individual way to learn how to give, and eventually to be a co-worker with God."

Chu-Tay's voice began to trail off as he said, *"True love is letting others have their own experience without interference or judgment. Baraka Bashad."*

After a few moments, I opened my eyes and Chu-Tay was there and Lena was just coming back to full awareness too. I said, "Chu-Tay, I have never heard the words *Baraka Bashad*. What does it mean?'

He replied, "It is an ancient blessing, and it means *may the blessings be*. In other words, everything is in God's care and we are content with that."

He got up and began to walk back to the hut.

"Would you two like some tea and biscuits?" he asked turning his head back to see us. We both said yes and followed him along the wide ledge and back into the hut. Seated on the floor with our tea, Chu-Tay looked at both of us and said, "You both know that there is no such thing as a coincidence, don't you?" Lena and I both looked at each other at the same time, smiled and nodded in agreement.

"You have been drawn here for the same purpose, and your paths have crossed for some very good reasons. I will help you with as much ancient wisdom as I feel you can benefit from. The rest is up to you. We all have to walk our own path and resolve our own karma."

With that Chu-Tay got up, pulled aside the door flap, and walked outside. Lena and I slowly got up and followed him outside a moment later. He was gone. We looked all around to be sure, but he was definitely gone. So we went back in to finish our tea and biscuit.

Both of us sat puzzled by this new message. I was thinking about his statement, "True love is letting others have their own experience without interference or judgment," when Lena broke into my thoughts: "Karma, I wonder what he meant by resolving karma?"

"We have been connected for a reason. There have been too many coincidences lately for me not to see this," I replied pensively. " First we both see Chu-Tay in our inner vision, then we both meet him here of all places. Then you and I meet, and I must confess, I feel a deep attraction for you....."

"And me to you," she broke in.

I reached for her hand to silently communicate that I appreciated her confirmation, and she let me hold it as I continued, "And we are able to feel relaxed with each other, and were able to share our life and our feelings over dinner, and then we realized that we have led parallel lives in many ways....."

"I'm so glad we have so much in common, Jack."

My heart was singing. There is something about the way she said my name. I felt so close to her the way she said it. My thoughts began to drift to planning the rest of the day and what to do. I reached over and took her other hand and spontaneously asked, "Lena, would you like to do some exploring today together?"

Lena beamed a bright smile, "I'm so glad you asked. I have a very comfortable feeling being with you Jack. I can't explain it, but I feel so very good when I'm with you."

Her words were so truthful, so refreshing. I wasn't used to such pure honesty. All of my past relationships with women were definitely not on the same foundation. Her statement was mirroring my thoughts in bed last night, and I agreed with her mentally before speaking: "You also make me feel very good when we are together. Last night at dinner, it was like our energy was in harmony. And I'm feeling it now. I feel more together, like I'm more complete when I am with you. It's hard to explain because I have not had feelings like this before. And even me saying this is amazing. I've never been able to share my feelings like this with a woman, but it feels so right with you. I feel like I can trust you."

She smiled and pulled me over to her and gave me a gentle lingering kiss on the lips and then pulled back. I was still feeling the sensations of what I can only describe as love flowing through my body, smelling her light wildflower perfume and feeling her hair against my cheek. I wanted to pull her toward me, but she was now pulling me up. She led me to the doorway before I could regain my emotional balance.

I pulled back the flap covering the door, and the bright morning sun was now filling the sky. The valley was almost fully lit below. We were still holding hands as I led the way, helping her down the steep rocky slope to the trail. On reaching the main trail, she slid her arm through mine as before, and we proceeded down to the ruins. I had the absolutely joyful Andre Bocelli song in my head, *Time To Say Goodbye*, as we walked along. I silently recalled some of the lyrics, *I know there is no light, in a room where the sun is not there, if you are not with me.* Lena was giving me the same feeling of joy that the song expressed for me. And then I wondered why I was recalling those words?

Chapter 9
Understanding Dreams

Lena and I spent a wonderful time together walking and talking among the ruins of the ancient city. We climbed up to the top of the observatory and sat in the middle of the ancient structure looking out over the small plaza at the top. Then we walked further over to the vast stone city all around holding hands all the while. Exploring around the four sides of the observatory, I pointed out to her the fourteen tiers that made up the pyramidal structure on the side where the observatory formed part of the outside city wall. I told her I thought the fourteen levels or tiers held some significance, but she could not offer any suggestions about what they might represent. We then walked down several staircases to the mid-level of the city and explored many buildings and rooms, marveling at the condition of the structures that, when discovered back in 1911, were covered in jungle.

The two of us spent a lot of time wandering hand-in-hand through streets of houses, towers, plazas, palaces, and terraces, all connected by staircases. As the sun hit the mid-day point, we strolled up and down more walkways and were able to check out the prisons, storehouses, and workshops. Continued investigation revealed a path, and we counted sixteen ceremonial baths that used to connect to a water channel which cascaded across the city. We were both intrigued by the carved stonework, the fountains and pillar details, as we studied the various niches. Together we then located the Temple of the Sun with its circular shape built over an enormous rock, and then happened on the cave beneath the Royal Tomb.

As we scouted out this lost Inca city, we both felt a wonderful sweet bond developing between us. She was so graceful and her voice so lilting, melodic to my ears, and her beauty was mirrored by such an inner glow, I didn't want to leave her alone. But she and I both knew we needed a little space. There was something about the ruins that fascinated the two of us, like we were almost there in the real city when it was the thriving nexus of the ancient Inca Empire.

We were both getting tired by the time we had examined the Three Window Temple, which was in excellent archeological condition. In the doorway of the temple, I gave her a long hug, and she put her head on my shoulder. My heart raced as I could feel her body pressing into mine. After a moment, she lifted her head a little, and we kissed tenderly for what felt like a moment in eternity. She pulled back a little and whispered, "That was amazing." I could only nod my head as I looked deeply into her shining crystal blue eyes.

We agreed to go our separate ways, but resolved to meet at eight o'clock at Lena's room for a Spiritual exercise together.

Within ten minutes I was back in my room and lay down on the bed for a rest. Thinking about all that had transpired between us that day, starting with our early morning visit with Chu-Tay, I made some journal notes. After a nap, I went down to the cafeteria and grabbed some dinner, eating in silence. I continued processing all that had happened with

Lena, recalling some of the things Chu-Tay had said. I even had a thought about what it would be like to live with her. I knew I needed to know her better to imagine that fully at this point, but I felt really good about the possibility.

Three hours later I knocked on the door at the appointed hour, and Lena welcomed me in with a gentle hug. I hugged her back, and gave her a brief kiss on the lips. She looked at me smiling and kissed me back, letting me know that her feelings were the same as mine. I sat down in the chair and she sat on the floor like the last time and I asked her if she knew the mantra, "Mahanta".

She smiled and exclaimed, "I have just learned this word a few days ago. It came to me on the inner during a contemplation!"

I said with joy, "Me too! Let's try it together?"

We both started together. Soon I was hearing violins and felt like I was enveloped in a golden light, with a feeling of great love pouring through all of my being. I then became aware of being in Chu-Tay's hut with Lena. We were seated together, holding hands and I held in my mind a question regarding the sound, "Mahanta."

Chu-Tay's voice spoke in the distance with a tone of humility, *"Mahanta is the spiritual name of the Master of Masters, an expression of the Spirit of God that is always with you."*

I could now understand why this sound had such a powerful effect.

My thoughts drifted to the dream Lena had shared with me. I had been curious about the dream, and it had been on my mind, as well as some of my own which I hadn't had an opportunity to share with her.

"Are dreams real? " I asked inwardly.
Chu-Tay began to speak again.
"The answer to the question is yes, but with a caveat" he replied.

"The two of you have had some important dreams in the last few days. When we sleep, the body is dormant and at rest. However, the inner aspect of us, our spiritual part, actually our real self called Soul is not. Soul is free to have experiences on the inner planes and indeed does "travel" to different places. Soul has at It's disposal the other bodies I talked about before in which to have these experiences.

It is these memories of our experiences in the inner worlds that constitute our dream memories. In their purest form these dream experiences are as real and as vivid as our experiences when we are awake. However, upon waking these memories of our inner world experiences are more often than not, jumbled thoughts and images. These inner journeys are occurring at different energy levels or vibratory rates that Soul can experience but are outside the perceptive abilities of the mind. When we visit the Astral Plane we are operating at the *next level or bandwidth. The Causal, the Mental, the Etheric and Soul Planes follow in order of vibratory rates as I have discussed with you before.*

I noticed my inner hearing was filling with my high-pitched electrical sound and my inner vision was surrounded with light in my peripheral vision.

When we visit the Astral worlds for example, we have a better chance of recalling these activities because we are operating in the closest vibratory proximity to our physical realm. The further we travel into the Spiritual worlds, the further we are from our physical vibration and therefore the more difficult it is to recall what happened. The experience has to be brought back through one plane at a time and then be processed by the mind.

Our mind has a built in censoring function that serves to protect us from information we are not ready for. This censor will jumble the visual images and substitute other images. And so many of your dreams can be a very jumbled collection of images. One can, however, with effort, bring a greater clarity to their dreams. In other words, we can begin to remember our experiences while operating as Soul on the other Spiritual Planes.

"How?" I questioned inwardly.

"By bringing a conscious effort to our spiritual development—by practicing a contemplation or spiritual exercise—this is the term I prefer—each day." he responded.

"When we commit ourselves to our spiritual growth we automatically increase our vibratory rate. We

are bringing ourselves into greater alignment and harmony with higher spiritual planes, the God Worlds. As this happens, our awareness expands and we become more in tune with all life. We start to see life from a higher perspective, that of Soul. As such we are better able to understand our true nature as Soul.

And so when Soul has experiences, we, in the physical body, are now operating in greater harmony with It. The vibratory gap narrows the more we align ourselves with Soul through our practice of spiritual exercises such as singing the word HU, Mahanta, and others. They serve to bring us closer to God."

Chu-Tay ended the "lesson" and the next thing I was aware of was the weight of my hands on the arms of the chair. I slowly stretched and opened my eyes. I couldn't help thinking again about the dream Lena had told me this morning about being in a small hut, feeling very unhappy, and then me leading her away running through the forest. It was such a clear dream for her and I wondered what it meant.

Lena and I got up silently. We hugged each other for a long time, and she gave me a sweet kiss which I returned. As we held each other, I felt like I didn't want to leave, but I knew that this relationship with Lena was different. My heart was telling me to take it slowly. I felt torn. My emotions wanted me to suggest that I stay, but my heart was telling me to be patient. I knew at a deep level that she was not a fleeting romance intention. Lena was stimulating in me a deep, more profound feeling; a kind of love that I'd never experienced before.

I didn't want to upset this connection we had discovered, so I pulled back a little from her and said, "Tomorrow morning at five-thirty?"

She smiled a big beautiful smile, gave me another lingering kiss and cheerfully whispered, "See ya!"

Chapter 10
Karma

It was five thirty and she walked right up to me, greeting me with a tender kiss as she ran her hand through my hair. I loved the feel of her fingers in my hair and her personal touch instantly made me feel she was as drawn to me as I was to her. I held her in my arms for a moment while my heart fluttered with a wonderful kind of joy as my neck and spine tingled with excitement. My spiritual exercise had given me a feeling that today would be a great day if I listened to my inner hearing and focused inwardly. When we parted I could see Lena was wearing a camouflage hiking jacket and pants that had a high fashion flare. She had her day pack on as well. It was just getting light enough to see the ground in the pre-dawn light. We slowly set out toward the slope and had just begun our climb on the trail at the base near the ruins, when Chu-Tay appeared in front of us, rounding a bend in the trail.

He greeted us saying, "Let's do something different today. Follow me if you will."

As the sky brightened a little, Chu-Tay led us into the ruins through the morning shadows along a wide walkway and up and down a couple of staircases. At this hour we were alone in the city, and it was especially quiet. We crossed a central plaza and passed a fountain, then carefully walked along a narrow walkway heading toward the other side. At an old building at the far edge of the site,

Chu-Tay disappeared inside the doorway, and I followed Lena through the entrance. Inside the light was very dim, but I could see that the walls were fairly smooth. I looked up and saw the last of the fading stars in the morning light, as the roofs had disappeared on all of the buildings long ago. Chu-Tay invited us to sit. Lena and I found a wide building block we could both fit on and sat down together. He positioned himself on a similar, smaller building stone in front of us and began to speak.

"I would like to touch on a spiritual principle that I raised before. It is the concept of karma, the principle of cause and effect. In other words, as ye sow, so shall ye reap."

We both began to sink into a deep contemplation as his words resonated in the walls of the ancient building.

"Karma is the prime vehicle for Soul's growth. Soul learns by experience, trial and error. Each lifetime, we incarnate into a body at birth and activate that body for our learning. And so we bring our past learning with us as Soul. No learning is lost and nothing is forgotten. Soul has a perfect "memory" of its responses to every moment of every lifetime experience. All of our actions, words, and even thoughts are recorded and form the basis of our continuing lessons and opportunity for growth. When we become aware of this in our human consciousness, we start to become cognizant of our responses to others. And we learn to discriminate, which means making right choices, responding to life from a higher viewpoint.

Our current life is a perfectly chosen set of lessons that we activate as we progress through our time in this world. We are given the opportunity to experience circumstances similar to those in which we have been before. And these experiences once again give us the opportunity to change the way we choose to respond in thought, word or deed. Our responses determine whether we can move on to other lessons or whether we need to repeat the lesson. We can often observe patterns in our own life and in the lives of others as we see circumstances repeating themselves. Some lessons—behaviors, attitudes, beliefs and emotions—can be difficult to modify or purify in one lifetime, and so the tests are repeated over the course of many incarnations, until learned.

There is no escape from our responsibility to ourselves as Soul and to our lessons. Karma is about understanding that whatever we have caused, whether good or not so good, will return to us in this lifetime or another for us to resolve. We resolve all experiences in terms of spiritual qualities that are the building blocks of our growth as Soul. We are continually becoming a purer vehicle for God's love"

As I listened to his words, I began to see a scene open in my inner vision, a scene in the ancient city where we were sitting. Lena and I were children in another time, and we were playing hide and seek. And then I could see myself hiding in a dark place. When I tried to get out I could not. I was locked in. I was terrified, and I thought I was going to die. After what seemed to be a few days, I was near death but the door opened and for a moment, I was blinded by the light, then I could see my childhood friend. She had found me, saved me. The vision slowly faded, and I became conscious of Chu-Tay's words as he continued.

"This world is considered to be ruled by five major traps, passions of the mind. These passions are negative behaviors that keep us circulating in this lower world called Earth, repeating lesson after lesson until we are ready to rise above the social or mass consciousness and take our true place as Spiritual Beings, co-working with God. These key negative passions, considered to be temptations are lust for persons or things, anger, greed, vanity and undue attachment to persons, ideas or things. These passions do have an opposite virtue and if we center our lives around them we can begin to "burn off" our karma and develop as beings, working for the good of the whole as opposed to solely for ourselves. These five virtues are discrimination, which is the art of choosing correctly, forgiveness, contentment, humility, and detachment."

Chu-Tay's voice began to fade as he concluded, *"By understanding this principle of karma or cause and effect, we can begin to focus on our responses to the circumstances of life using the five virtues."*

As we came back to our physical awareness, I wanted to tell Chu-Tay about my vivid experience, but he was gone. I turned to Lena and tears were streaming down her face. She was shaking, so I moved over as close as I could get to comfort her. I put my arm around her and she put her head on my shoulder. I let her settle down for a couple of minutes, then asked if she would like to talk.

"I had a vision of being there in the ancient city," she began. "It was as clear as I see right now. You were there too. We were in love and wanted to marry but my father had selected another for me to marry and I could not convince him otherwise. I was heartbroken that we could not be together. I lived a very unhappy life without you."

We got up slowly and I told her about my inner experience with her when we were young children there, as well, and that she had saved my life. She looked at me, staring deeply into my eyes, and then gave me a beautiful soft kiss. We stood there hugging each other for what seemed to be about five minutes as she rested her head on my shoulder, sobbing, consumed by the emotion of connecting with such a profound experience.

As the sun began to illuminate the mountain tops, I led her out of the building, through the ruins and back to the lobby of the lodge. We decided we both needed time to think about our experiences. So we agreed to go our separate ways for the rest of the day and to meet for dinner at five o'clock.

Lena headed up to her room and I went straight for the cafe for a big breakfast of pancakes and coffee. Then I went back to my room, grabbed my journal and made some notes for about a half hour. Next, I turned my attention to what to do for the day. I reviewed some literature, looked at the options and decided to hike up the Inca trail, as I had not been past the *Gate of the Sun*.

After getting some snack food and water, I set out in the morning sun. It was shirtsleeves temperature on the trail. I reached the *Gate of the Sun* and stopped briefly to take a last glance at the ancient city in the distance. Proceeding onward, I followed the ancient route for about two hours.

The trail seemed relatively easy compared to my hike up Wayna Picchu, but then I met two tired-looking trekking groups headed toward Machu Picchu, and I wondered what lay ahead.

It was a great day and the trail turned out to be only a moderate degree of difficulty in the section I was hiking. It gave me time to think and process much of what had transpired in meeting Lena and what she had told me about her vision. It was amazing to learn we were in love in another time but unable to marry. I also thought about my own vision in the ancient city while Chu-Tay was speaking to us. I now felt with certainty that Machu Picchu had been my home in another lifetime. It explained many of the feelings I had, but opened up many other questions which remained unanswered in my mind.

As I headed back along the trail, I couldn't wait to explore all the possibilities with Lena over dinner.

Chapter 11
Spiritual Growing Pains

I was five minutes early for dinner and asked to be seated by the window again. My heart was fluttering with the anticipation of seeing Lena. I couldn't wait. I wanted her tell me about her day and I wanted to talk about our morning spiritual experiences, the visions that opened up to each of us while listening to Chu-Tay in the building in the ruins. The waiter filled my water glass, and I asked him to bring me a slice of lemon for it as well. She was late, but she could be late. That was okay with me, I thought.

By ten after five, I had scanned the restaurant several times to see if she was sitting somewhere else, but she was not in the restaurant. At quarter after five I was starting to really wonder where she was. She had been so punctual for our other meetings early in the morning and for our first dinner. This didn't seem to be like her. But then again, we were just getting to know each other and, could I be sure about her? As I sat there staring out the window, the waiter came over to take my order but I explained to him that I was waiting for a friend.

"She must have been held up," I said.

As time rolled on, I began to wonder if she had been really upset with the experience that morning. Maybe she was even standing me up! The thought rolled into my head like a heavy cloud, but I pushed it back out. No, I said to myself, Lena was different. We had made a connection, and I had to trust that feeling. But perhaps she was frightened by the experience? By six o'clock I was beginning to think she had just gotten the time wrong and that she would be down any minute. So I sat waiting, looking out the window, trying not to feel like the man in the restaurant scene in the Steve Martin movie, *The Lonely Guy*. But a strange sinking feeling crept into me. Somehow I knew better. I was denying reality, but I couldn't believe she was standing me up on purpose.

At six fifteen, I decided to order as the waiter was starting to press me, but my appetite was gone. My dinner came so quickly, it seemed like the waiter had cooked it himself, so he could free the table for others now in line. I forced down some soup and salad and only ate half of my chicken, paid the bill and left. I didn't know whether to be angry or upset as I walked down the hall to the lobby. Maybe I was feeling a bit of both. I stopped at the front desk and learned that her room key was still there. She had not returned! I felt my stomach tighten. I asked the receptionist to call her room, just in case, but there was no answer. Now I was worried, and my feelings of betrayal faded into the background as my concern rose. I wrote a note for her, asking her to call my room any time in the night to let me know she was back and OK. I asked the receptionist to give it to her when she came in.

I headed back up to my room and sat on the bed, just thinking about what could have happened. She had probably gone down to Agues Calientes in the valley below to do some shopping like she had done the other day. Maybe she missed the last bus back, or maybe she met someone, maybe an old friend? Perhaps she forgot about our arrangement for dinner and decided to eat in the town? All these thoughts entered my head, but I resolved in my mind not to get too concerned. There was probably a rational explanation for the whole thing.

I got ready for bed, but I could not shake the anxious feeling in my gut as I climbed into bed. It took me a half hour to get to sleep, chewing over my missed dinner with Lena and the excitement I had felt all day about seeing her again. It was the first thing on my mind when my wake-up call brought me out of my dreams at five a.m.

August 19

I rolled out of bed in my pajamas, sat in the chair and began my morning spiritual exercise to settle my thoughts about Lena. After about ten minutes singing HU, I fell into a silent contemplation. It was during this quiet period of listening and looking that I got a flash, a sort of impression of Lena. She was upset and in a dark place. I continued with my contemplation and toward the end, I asked for inner clarification of what I had seen, but all I received was a strong feeling that something was very wrong.

I showered and shaved, got dressed and went downstairs. I checked with the front desk and they confirmed that Lena's key had not been picked up and my note was still there for her. My heart sank. I had a strong feeling of foreboding, that she needed my help. At this moment I could only think of seeing Chu-Tay. He would know. Maybe Lena was there with him? Maybe she had been there all along, I thought, but in a way I also knew I was kidding myself.

In the early morning light, I slowly picked my way along the trail and when I reached the *Gate of the Sun*, the light was getting bright enough to navigate the steep incline to Chu-Tay's hut. Chu-Tay greeted me in his usual manner, but he did not ask about Lena. It seemed like he knew she would not be with me. He was not at all surprised that I was alone. He held back the door flap and invited me in, and sure enough Lena was not there. He asked me to sit down and offered me tea, which I accepted in the same tin cup. I was anxious, and I was getting ready to give him the news, but as I gathered up myself to talk about Lena's absence, I somehow felt that he was going to offer me an explanation. He began to speak before I could ask him.

"Jack, you are here for your greater unfoldment and so is Lena. You two have much to give each other, and sometimes there are things that must be worked out for the greater benefit of Soul. I can see you are anxious about her. There are some people who seem to live enchanted lives in this world. And we are also able to see pain and suffering all around the world. The question many ask is 'Why must there be so much pain?'

There is a broad spectrum of consciousness on Earth reflected in the billions of people living here, and what we are really seeing when we see all these different experiences that others are having, is Soul in various settings, growing in Its awareness of Spiritual Principles or laws. Before we incarnate again, we are able to view, as Soul, our chosen path in this lifetime and understand the broad challenges that the new lifetime and its setting will offer to us as Soul for our growth.

And so it is not for us to judge others and the experience they are having. Right now Lena is having an experience that she needs for her growth.

Soul inherently has the ability to solve all of Its challenges. Often, all it needs is a listening ear. We learn that we are not here to solve the problems of others. Nor can we, and have them benefit from their challenges as Soul. We usually have enough of our own. And if we choose to get involved in finding solutions for others, we can actually take on their problems. This is called taking on the karma of another. And so we learn to help by helping others solve their own problems with compassion.

Pain and suffering in this world is not God's fault. We must take responsibility for our lives, and there is no time like the present. We can change our lives by this very action of accepting responsibility. By doing this we set in motion an array of circumstances that will alter our lives because we are opening ourselves to new possibilities. We begin to flow with life instead of resisting it. The resistance is what causes us pain. Flowing with the rhythm of life is to work with Soul's natural urges to have the experiences that it has chosen for this lifetime. Listening to Soul is the most joyful way to live and grow because Soul will have Its way. And listening to the inner voice becomes a tool for our survival.

After a long pause, Chu-Tay stated,

Jack, Lena is in trouble, but I cannot help you outwardly. You will have to work with your inner hearing, connecting with your inner guidance, and she will have to as well. You can connect to this guidance through nudges, intuition, insights, or even a feeling of love.

This is your experience, and hers, as painful as it may be. My heart goes with you on your journey. You can find me in your spiritual exercises for guidance on the principles that are manifesting in these present circumstances."

There were those words again. I was now more anxious than ever as Chu-Tay had confirmed my worst fears. Lena was in trouble. But what kind of trouble?

"Jack, use your intuition, contemplation, be watchful, and listen and you will succeed. Baraka Bashad."

I opened my eyes to question Chu-Tay some more about Lena, but he was gone. I felt a terrible feeling creep into the core of my being as I slowly got up and moved outside the hut. I had learned one key fact: Lena was in trouble. Chu-Tay had confirmed my earlier experience from my spiritual exercise; the flash of seeing Lena upset and in a dark place. I felt my head was spinning. What was I to do? What could I do?

I sat down on a rock outcrop because I felt too wobbly to stand, and I shivered a little with emotion in the cool morning air. The anxious feeling in my gut had become a knot. I subconsciously looked over the ancient city which was just starting to be illuminated, building-top by building-top in the morning sun. Chu-Tay's words were still in my mind; We can change our lives by accepting responsibility," and "Listening to the inner voice becomes a tool for our survival." As I recalled bits and pieces of his message, I was wondering what all this meant to me and Lena. How could this help?

A few minutes later I got up, lost in thought, and picked my way carefully down the steep slope to the trail. Then something Chu-Tay said registered with me: "I cannot help you outwardly." And then he said, "You can find me in your spiritual exercises for guidance on the principles that are manifesting in these present circumstances." I got a chill of recognition as it dawned on me that he can help me, but

I sensed that he was asking me to meet him half way! The realization made me feel a little more buoyant and gave me a sense of direction. I reached the trail and started to head down toward the lodge. Just then a group of about ten very tired-looking trekkers arrived from somewhere out there on the ancient Inca Highway at the *Gate of the Sun* to observe the famous sunrise over the lost city.

A new day was dawning, and I sensed the symbolism of the deeper meaning of Chu-Tay's message that was "dawning" on me!

Chapter 12
The Spiritual Meaning of Love

I went straight back to the reception desk to see if Lena had returned, but her key was still there. I decided to have the manager check her room to make sure she wasn't there. I explained my concerns to the receptionist at the front desk, and then she disappeared through a door behind the reception. I waited for about five minutes. She returned with a graying, tall, stately gentleman who she introduced as Senor Manuel Attunes, the General Manager of the lodge. He looked grave as I explained the circumstances and described how Lena looked.

"A beautiful woman? Missing?" he questioned sternly. "Yes senor, let's have a look at her room immediately."

I followed him up to her room. He pulled out his pass key and opened the door. We found all of Lena's things still there. Her back pack was gone, and there was no sign of her purse or money. It looked to me like she had not come back in the afternoon as she still had all of her evening dinner clothes hung up. As I stood there trying to make sense of the situation, I began to feel that this was most unusual of her to have not come back to her room. It all seemed to add up to what I'd been denying for the last hour. Chu-Tay's words rang in my head, "Lena is in trouble." My heart was starting to ache, and my face must have shown it too.

I looked at senor Attunes and he said, "I am sorry she is not here. Would you like to make a report to the police?"

"Yes, where is the nearest station?" I responded, grateful for the suggestion.

"At the bottom of the valley in Agues Calientes," he replied. "Would you like me to make a call, Senor?"

"Yes, please tell them I'm coming down as soon as I can get there. It's the pale green building on the main street isn't it?

"Si Senor, It's near where the train tracks end."

I stopped and looked at the Manager and confided, somewhat embarrassed, "You know, Lena and I have just met—four days ago, but I don't know her last name. We never got around to discussing last names."

"Under the circumstances I will tell you her name—it is Sandberg," he smiled. "She is registered here as Lena Sandberg."

"Thank you so much," I replied as I moved out the door. I felt compelled to move quickly. Now that I knew what to do next, I didn't want to waste any time. My instinct, though, was telling me that there may be another way.

I ran up the stairwell two steps at a time, not wanting to wait for the elevator, got to my room and grabbed some things, including my passport and the map the receptionist had given me. I chucked them into my back pack and headed out of the lodge. I walked quickly toward the buses lined up to take tourists back down the mountain after their tour of the site. I was alone on the bus, as everyone was just coming up from town for the day. I sat up front to see the road as the driver sees it, more to keep my equilibrium as I was feeling light-headed at the thought of Lena being in trouble.

The bus took off at exactly quarter past ten and wound its way down the hairpin turns. On every one, I could see straight down to the bottom of the mountain and the Urubamba River rapids below. The driver had to guide the wheels within inches of the edge of the gravel road for the bus to make it around most of the tight turns. It took my mind off Lena's disappearance for a few minutes, and I was glad for the mental diversion.

I flew off the bus and jogged up the street to the flat-roofed pale green police station, through the open door and up to the counter. A short round-faced native-looking officer came out of a back room and walked up to me on the other side of the counter. He had been expecting me and immediately asked for my passport. I handed it to him and he disappeared into a back room. I stood there for what seemed like twenty minutes wondering what was going on. I was so keyed up that I started walking around the room looking at notices on the walls in Spanish, trying to read the words to take my mind off waiting. He finally returned with a large, more-Spanish looking officer who I found out later was the commander of the detachment. The officer shook my hand, smiled and asked me to follow him into his office.

After I had sat down in an old wooden chair in front of his gray metal desk, he frowned and asked, "Senor, you are a friend of the lady named Lena Sandberg?"

"Yes, we met four days ago and have become friends and I am now worried because she hasn't returned to her room at the lodge! All her clothes seem to be still there."

"Si," agreed the commander, "your story is the same as that of Manuel Attunes, the lodge Manager who is also my cousin." He turned to the junior officer and uttered a few words in Spanish and he quickly left the office and shut the door behind him. The commander focused his attention back on me and with a very serious look said, "Senor, when was the last time you saw your friend?"

I replied," Yesterday morning in the ruins of Machu Picchu."

The commander frowned, which made me a little nervous. He looked me directly in the eyes and asked, "What was she wearing?"

I visualized Lena in the ruins and responded, "She was wearing a camouflage hiking jacket and pants, and she had her day pack with her as well."

He made some notes on a form for about thirty seconds, and I could feel my stomach beginning to knot. He abruptly looked up and flatly stated, "Senor, we have some bad news to give you. Your friend has been kidnapped."

I was momentarily stunned. "What!" I exclaimed, "Who would want to do such a thing?

"Like every other country, there are those here that do not want to work honestly for a living." he replied. "Your friend is being held for a ransom and we are taking steps to contact her father."

The commander explained that Lena's father owned a large steel company in Sweden and that the kidnappers had done their homework well. He added that she was in grave danger, as hostages have been known to disappear in these circumstances if there are delays in payment, and that they were asking for one million US dollars. He abruptly stood up and said, "Senor, there is nothing you can do. We do not agree with rewarding crimes and do not approve of paying any ransoms but sometimes people take matters into their own hands, if you know what I mean. We have been in touch with our national security branch in Lima regarding this matter, and they will be handling this most unfortunate situation. Please come back tomorrow, and we may have news of her father's intentions and from our investigations in this matter."

Still in shock and back out on the street, I stood there wondering what to do next. I felt like I had been hit by a truck. I seemed to have come to a dead end, and there appeared to be nothing else I could do. After standing there for a few minutes, inwardly shaking, I started walking up the main street along the railroad tracks and sat down at the first outdoor cafe. The tables were wooden, with wooden chairs and green table clothes, and each was set with a small vase of fresh flowers. It looked very inviting. I sat under the awning and was able to position myself just out of the bright late morning sun. I ordered a coffee and some breakfast, and when I finished picking at my food, I just sat there thinking about what I could do. I was in no hurry. Where was I going, anyway?

As the trauma wore off, I became very concerned about her safety. In a half daze, I blankly studied the main street. The dual set of railroad tracks separated one side of the street from the other, and a little yellow maintenance rail car was making its way along one of the tracks. The merchants began opening their craft stalls and stores for the day, positioning their colorful shawls and hats and other items to catch the eyes of the tourists as they walked by from the bus terminal to the hotels and lodges in the center of town. At the end of the street, the green wall of the almost vertical mountain formed a backdrop.

After finishing my coffee and still lost in thought, I remembered Chu-Tay's words about the HU and how it could help in times of trouble. I decided the best thing I could do was go back to my room and try to calm down with a spiritual exercise. I slowly walked back to the bus terminal and this time had to stand in line for the next bus leaving, as it seemed like all the tourists in town were now heading up to Machu Picchu for the day. Within forty minutes I entered the lodge just outside the gates of the lost city, and as I passed by the reception, conversations went quiet. I could sense the staff looking at me with deep concern. It seemed that they now knew about Lena too. I turned my head and caught a glimpse of two men in suits talking to a staff member in the back room.

Back in my room, I got myself comfortable and began to sing HU. As I was emotionally distraught, it took me a long time to begin to move into a deep attunement with my inner being. But after a while I began to hear the sound of rushing water, and I knew I was beginning to rise above my anxiety and the shock of hearing about Lena's kidnapping. I wanted to gain a higher perspective, and Chu-Tay had said that if I could use my intuition, I could possibly help. But how? I decided to ask inwardly for help in my contemplation.

The blue light that had appeared to me on just a few occasions, started to enter my inner vision. It was a brilliant, almost electric blue, and the sound changed to the sound of violins, playing in the distance. A scene opened up for me in my inner vision, and like a clear dream, I saw Lena tied to a bed in a hut. And then I could see many men and tents by a cabin near a river. My love deepened for her as I felt my heart break at her captivity and the look of fear on her face. The scene faded and I began to hear Chu-Tay's words speak to me.

"Love is a very powerful thing. It is timeless and stretches across all boundaries. The love I am re-ferring to is Divine love. The Creator loves me and you unconditionally. This love is so great that the Creator has formed you and me as Soul and has set us on our eternal journeys to become God-like, to take on Its qualities. God loves me, you and ev-ery other Soul with an equal amount of love. There are no limits to this love. The love that I have for you is like God's love for all of us. I love you uncon-ditionally. I accept you the way you are. You can make errors so to speak, but these errors are for your growth.

God does not forgive because It does not judge in the first place. I offer you this same love in pro-viding you inner guidance today as a vehicle for the Mahanta; to create your life with my support but with complete freedom. In fact, I wish you the best in whatever you decide in this difficult situa-tion, because my love is comprised of offering you divine freedom. Love is a true caring for the other and for their welfare. But its quality is empathy, not sympathy. Empathy is caring and an involvement only by invitation. Sympathy is an involvement that often constitutes a judgment of some kind. And so this journey we are all on is about learning how to truly love.

Like the growth of Soul, there is always one more step. Jack, I invite you to see that your goals, the end points, are less and less important to life and move to a moment-to-moment focus, thus making the journey the purpose of your life. In this way you can tune in better and help your friend. Serving all life takes on true meaning as loving all life. It means giving others time and attention by listening, and by looking for opportunities to silently serve others. The process of growing spiritually is accelerated by selfless giving and when we give, we receive sacred gifts to bring us closer to experiencing the Divine in our life at all times.

It is love that connected the two of you before this lifetime and it has the power to bring you together again."

I slowly came back to my waking state, and after a minute, opened my eyes. I perceived a profound sense of balance and calmness. The spiritual exercise had helped me shift to the higher state of being that Chu-Tay had been talking about. I sat there thinking about his words with a new sense that I could do something for Lena, and that we would see each other again. I resolved that I had to do all I could to find Lena myself by working with my inner awareness.

I reflected back on his words, "I invite you to see that your goals, the end points are less and less important, and move to a moment-to-moment focus, thus making the journey the purpose of your life."

My goal was to find Lena. I asked myself, what he meant by, "moment-to moment focus." The answer jumped into my consciousness, ASK AND LISTEN FOR GUIDANCE. Chu-Tay was with me; he is guiding me, I realized! I recalled his words, "I offer you this same love in providing you inner guidance today as a vehicle for the Mahanta." The thought impressions I had just received were as strong as hearing spoken words. All I need to do is work with this new tool, to trust what I am "hearing," I thought!

Then I reflected on the vision I had perceived after seeing the blue light, the flash of Lena being tied to a bed in a hut. Lena had dreamed of being in a hut too, I recalled. But she had also dreamed that I was leading her away through the forest.

Chapter 13
Letting Go

I decided that I needed some air and went for a long afternoon stroll in the ruins, walking up and down pathways and worn staircases and exploring more buildings. It seemed amazing to me how well I could remember where different buildings were after my previous tour on my own and then with Lena. It felt like a language I had not used since childhood coming back to me as I intuitively knew what was around every corner. After an hour, I climbed to the top of the observatory and sat there for a long time reflecting on all of the events that had occurred since leaving St. Louis. I felt life had sped up in a way.

As the sun was arching to the west, hovering near the top of a mountain, I slowly made my way down and over to the lodge. It was late afternoon, and I was getting very hungry. I walked down the hall to the dining room and found it was open and serving a few Germans from a tour group, so I decided to have my dinner. I ate a roast beef dish with potatoes that reminded me of home, and then I headed back to my room. The day had taken its toll on me, and I was emotionally exhausted. I lay down on the bed to read, but soon found I could not keep my eyes open, so I got ready for bed and then crashed. Sleep came fast.

I awoke with a start in the middle of the night with a frightening dream fresh in my head and sweat running down my forehead.

I was a child locked in a very tight and dark place. I could hardly breathe and I was scared. After a long time the box opened and there was my friend. I had the feeling that it was Lena, but she was a young girl my age in the dream.

I grabbed the notepad on my bedside table and jotted the dream down so I could remember it in the morning. I lay back down in bed and calmed down by singing HU a few times. After a few minutes I finally was able to get back to sleep.

August 20

I woke up early. I realized I had gone to sleep early, at seven-thirty last night. It was still pitch black outside at four o'clock but I couldn't sleep anymore, so I got up. I took my time with my shower and shave, then sat down to do my spiritual exercise. I picked up my note pad and reviewed the dream I had jotted down in the night. It seemed to be linked to my other spiritual experience, the vision I had while Chu-Tay was speaking to Lena and I in the ruins—about being locked in a dark, small space—and I resolved to ask for greater clarity about its meaning.

A few minutes into the exercise I began to hear my familiar inner sound and I became aware of a deeper sense of perspective, a shift in awareness. I asked about the dream that had wakened me in the middle of the night. The impression came back to me that it <u>was</u> the same experience I had in contemplation while listening to Chu-Tay in the ruins the other day. I had the understanding that Spirit was trying to move this awareness into my conscious mind. I continued to listen to the inner sounds for another several minutes, and then I ended my morning exercise. I knew, on coming back to physical awareness that I would ask Chu-Tay for guidance this morning.

I set out a little earlier, about five-twenty, the sky still filled with stars but showing a little light. I picked my way along the trail, being careful not to trip on the odd rock that stuck out on the ancient pathway. As I reached the *Gate of the Sun*, the pre-dawn sky was getting brighter, and it was easy to see the best foot placements on the steep climb up to the hut. Reaching the ledge I called out, "Good Morning, Chu-Tay"

"Come inside, Jack."

As I lifted the flap aside I could see Chu-Tay by the fire just putting on a pot of tea. He said quietly and in a calm voice, "Good morning, Jack. I can see that you are upset and you have some questions. Perhaps I can help you better understand."

"Yes, I have many questions about everything that has happened with you, Chu-Tay. But the most important one is about Lena. Can you tell me where she is and how I can help her?"

He thought for a moment as I sat down. I watched him put some biscuits on the fire. He poured me some tea and said, "The biscuits will be ready in just a few minutes." He continued, changing his tone:

"One of the aspects of love that we can apply to everyday life is letting go.

It was easier to close my eyes when Chu-Tay talked, and this morning was no exception.

Even in dire circumstances, if you truly love someone, you are willing to let them find their destiny in whatever way they desire, and this includes letting them go.

Surrender to the larger invisible agenda of Soul is the key. Surrender. A first step is to recognize that Soul has the last word in all of our life challenges and problems. It is important to recognize that we do need our minds, but it is how we use the mind that is important. The mind is great at setting goals and working through details but the shift to operating from Soul is to set the mind free of the final outcome. This is called letting go. Once we have set a process in motion, it will manifest in some way, and in reality the mind is powerless to force the outcome. It is up to Soul and Divine Will. So why not let all outcomes manifest this way? The benefits are amazing. Having no attachment to outcomes is a very free way of living. There is no stress when we allow our lives to manifest in harmony with Divine Will.

There is an expression that sums this up: "My will or Thy will be done."

When we say "My will be done," we are trying to force a desired outcome that the mind has conceived. When we say "Thy will be done," we are surrendering the outcome to Divine Spirit. This is the secret to creating our lives in a gentle and beautiful way. Turning our life over to our higher self is to live in harmony with our true self and the universe."

His voice began to trail off as he said, *"Some call this following the heart."*

I was holding the tin tea mug, still steaming as I opened my eyes. I looked down, and there in front of me was a metal plate with three hot biscuits. Chu-Tay was gone. I sat there sipping my tea and took a bite out of a biscuit. I realized that I had wanted to know more about Lena but he was gone before I could ask. I mulled over in my mind his last words, "following the heart." Yes, I determined, I was going to follow my heart, and my heart was with Lena. I recognized how deeply in love with her I felt! And as I thought and felt this, my heart filled with joy at the sudden recognition of this love in me. I had never felt this kind of love before. It felt genuine. True. Pure. I could not describe it in any other way.

I knew now that I would do anything for her. I must get her back, safely. I must follow my heart. It almost felt like a double entendre, to follow my heart. I would follow my love, but I would also work with my heart, my feelings and intuition. Chu-Tay's message resonated back to me: he had said, "Soul has the last word in all of our life challenges." I remembered that he'd also said this before; that I would have to work with my inner hearing, my spiritual tools. And then just a minute ago he had said something about, "surrendering the outcome to Divine Spirit."

I finished all three biscuits, washing them down with my now warm tea, then I got up and walked out into the brilliant, rising sun. I picked my way down the steep slope to the trail, and then I walked down the Inca Trail to Machu Picchu, thinking deeply about his words. I resolved to do what I could to find Lena, but I would turn over the outcome to Spirit. I felt a lot more relaxed as I came to this resolution, knowing that I was now headed in the right direction—an inner direction.

Chu-Tay had said that it was Lena's challenge too, but I also felt I could help her if I worked with spiritual tools as well as my natural investigative research skills I'd developed as a stock broker.

Chapter 14
Waking Dreams

When I got to Machu Picchu I decided to pass on having breakfast right away and head all the way down to the police station in Agues Calientes for any word. I waited a half hour, and then caught the first bus down after it dropped off the early bird tourists at the top near the site. The sun was just reaching the bottom of the valley when I arrived at the terminal area. I walked up the still quiet main street and when I arrived at the police station, the commander was at the front desk smiling as I approached.

"I wanted to see if you had any news," I said trying to sound hopeful.

"Senor," he replied overly calmly, "We have just heard from our national security headquarters, and they have no leads. They have had several men investigating throughout the area, and the information you provided is about as much as they have learned, although she was sighted here in the town in the afternoon. Also, they have been unable to reach the father. According to his company he is on vacation in a remote part of Tibet doing some mountain climbing. His firm is trying to reach him and are doing everything they can, but I'm afraid we are running out of time. The kidnappers like to work fast. Please come back tomorrow, and we may have other news."

I couldn't believe my ears. This was serious. They have no leads, and her father can't be reached! The commander's words, "the kidnappers like to work fast," echoed in my head. I knew now this was up to me, and I felt a twinge in my chest. I remembered Chu-Tay's words and tried to let the outcome go: I could sense that if I got too wound up, my intuition would close down. I knew that working with my inner tools was the only way I could help.

I left the police station and looked up and down the street. The town was peaceful in the early morning sun and none of the cafes looked open, so I just stood there wondering what to do. Only one thing came to mind—go back to the lodge and do another Spiritual exercise to see if I could get a glimpse of Lena.

I walked back to the terminal. More early morning tourists were getting on one of the first busses, their only destination being the top of Machu Picchu. I found a seat about three quarters of the way back. After a few minutes we were on our way, grinding up the long and winding road. As I thought about this, I remembered the Beetles song, *The Long and Winding Road* and started humming the words to myself.

> *The long and winding road,*
> *That leads to your door,*
> *Will never disappear,*
> *I've seen that road before,*
> *It always leads me here,*
> *Leads me to your door.*

I thought to myself, maybe the words are telling me something? I was lost in thought as the bus reached the terminal at the top, and I still could not see what the words meant for me, but they felt comforting in a strange way. I ambled up to the lodge and noticed that the cafeteria was only half-full. I had an inner nudge to get my breakfast now rather than after my exercise. As I entered the dining room, I could feel several concerned and anxious eyes follow me to my table, and I sensed that Lena's kidnapping was now common knowledge, creating a concern among the lodge guests. I was seated right away and within a minute the waiter filled my glass with fresh squeezed orange juice. Although I was not hungry at all, I knew I must eat to maintain my strength to help Lena. I ordered eggs, bacon, and toast, which also came quickly. By the time I had finished, the room was almost jammed full with tour groups and couples, and I thought to myself, that was another good decision, to follow my intuition to eat first. I resolved to listen inwardly more and to be flexible in the moment to nudges and opportunities.

Back in my room, I settled into my chair and began my spiritual exercise in the usual way, singing HU. After a few minutes I shifted to singing "Mahanta." I remembered Chu-Tay saying this meant master of masters. I had been given some amazing spiritual experiences with the Light and Sound in the last few days with this new word. I began to hear my usual high pitched electrical sound, and I followed it for a few minutes as I sang, feeling very relaxed and open to the experience this morning. Another sound began to emerge, the sound of bells tinkling in the distance, and then a soft golden light entered my inner vision. After several moments I could see the face of Lena in the light, then her hands which were outstretched to me. The vision lasted but for a second or two, and I could almost smell her scent, the light wildflower perfume she had about her. Her face slowly faded, and I could hear Chu-Tay's voice as his words came clearly into my consciousness.

"Spirit talks to us—all the time, Jack. Waking dreams are one way to listen. They are occurring all of the time. They are actually God speaking

to us. We only have to pay attention. In fact, the best way of tuning in to waking dreams is to know that they are occurring moment-to-moment and to expect them.

"What are they?" I silently asked.

"They are spiritual insights, events that stand out from the rest of life and can give us tips or guid- ance in dealing with life. Observing is the key— taking notice of the waking dreams, the intuitions and the nudges, and paying attention to our dreams. And so the little events in our lives begin to have greater meaning. Taking a wrong turn while driving can mean that you have taken a 'wrong turn' in some other aspect of your life. Lost keys can mean that you need to search for a key to solve another problem, and drivers honking at you can let you know that you must pay atten- tion in another area of your life. Even seeing a bird or an animal or hearing a song on the radio or in your head can be a waking dream and offer meaning and direction.

All of this guidance is a tremendous gift and can help solve and even avoid so called problems. Life can be much smoother, less hectic, with few- er surprises, and you can be better prepared for handling the big challenges."

His words drifted off, and I thought about *The Long and Winding Road* Beetles song I was humming on the bus. Per- haps it was telling me that I would be led to Lena's door! For a minute, I stayed with that positive thought and the feeling and confidence I felt in the moment. And then my mind drifted back to the circumstances of how I got to Peru in the first place. Seeing Machu Picchu in my contemplations, the radio show caller, and then just being outside the Flight Center at that very moment when they had flights to Lima on sale. And Jim, my branch manager, being at the office later than usual when I called so he could give me the go ahead. I could see a perfectly organized set of events and I could easily accept what Chu-Tay was talking about.

I was hoping for specific answers from Chu-Tay, but now I realized that his answers <u>were</u> direct, just a different kind of "direct" that let me understand certain principles for myself. I now knew with certainty that I had to take responsibility and meet him half way, working with my spiritual tools as well as my investigative skills, and then the answers would come.

I reached for my journal and made some notes for about a half hour. Then I got up out of my chair and resolved to look for the clues, the waking dreams, as well as work with my nudges and spiritual exercises to find Lena.

Chapter 15
Harmony and Divine Will

As I entered the dining room around eleven thirty, I could feel the tension among the guests, no doubt the result of the presence of the national security investigators and their questioning of staff and guests. I ordered lunch as several people scrutinized me and then continued their hushed conversations.

Over lunch, I had the opportunity to mull over all of the recent realizations. I began to feel the need to get myself in motion, to do some exploring and clue hunting. I remembered seeing some trekkers coming into town near the bus terminus in the valley below, and I began to feel like that would be a good starting point for the afternoon. I went back to my room, dug around in my pack, and found the map the receptionist had given me. Sure enough, there was a line that looked like a trail in the valley below leading from the town over toward the base of Wayna Picchu. It had to be a trail, as there were no roads anywhere, I decided. I put a water bottle in my day pack as well as my Cardinals hat and a light jacket, just in case. Who knows what could happen in spite of the perfect eighty degree temperatures in the valley? I decided I needed to be open to whatever turns in the road came up.

As I left the lodge for the bus down into town once more, I set out with the thought of paying attention to anything that would offer me a clue to Lena's whereabouts. I was getting used to the twenty-minute bus trip now, the fact that I could see to the bottom, and the river rapids below. The little boy was now in action for the afternoon. This added another note of interest for me; not only watching him, but the reaction of the other tourists seeing him, for the first time, perform his superhuman feat. He raced straight down the mountain on his impossibly steep trail and greeted the bus with his waves and shouts. He caught their attention and gave them quite a show, to their amazement. The bus appeared to be mostly one group from England, judging from their accents. They applauded and cheered, "Bravo!" each time the boy appeared, shouting and waving his arms at the bus.

At the bottom, the boy got on the bus and passed his hat, and the smiling and laughing Brits filled it with English pound notes and Peruvian soles notes and coins. I got a bill out and decided to speak to the boy once outside the bus.

"Buenos dias," I greeted him. I put a dollar bill in his hat after the rest had finished rewarding him. He smiled a big smile with some missing teeth and said, "Gracias. You American?" he asked. "I love America. I want to go there one day."

I was delighted he spoke some English and asked, "Is there a trail in the valley near here?"

"Si, Senor American. I will show you. Come this way"

He quickly led me, jogging a hundred yards down to the end of the roadway. Where it terminated, I noticed there was a trail entering the dense greenery that looked well used. He smiled and pointed saying "It goes through the valley and then goes up Wayna Picchu. It is not too much difficult, not like the top."

I reached in my pocket for another dollar bill, but he had already turned and started running to the bus to catch a ride back up to the top of the mountain, I suspected, for another run down the mountain.

"Gracias," I yelled behind him.

The trail was a beautiful hike through lush tropical valley foliage that led over to Wayna Picchu, just the level of activity I was hoping for; not too easy and not too blood-chilling. When I reached the base, the trail rose up the rock face in steps and started to require some serious energy to climb. I stopped to catch my breath and looked back a few times so that I could see the town of Agues Calientes from different vantage points until the trail took me out of site around the back side of the mountain. As I proceeded upward, the trail continued to get narrower and difficult to navigate in the odd place, but nowhere as harrowing as the top section I had climbed. Up ahead, I thought I could hear voices, and then quiet. Then voices again, this time for certain. I rounded a corner and there were three hikers, two women and a man in their late sixties or seventies that looked like seasoned hikers with hiking sticks, professional hiking boots and double water bottle holders on their packs.

As we met on the narrow trail, I stopped and said in greeting, "Hello. Beautiful day for a hike."

The man and one of the women answered cheerfully, almost in unison, "Bonjour," in a French accent.

I asked, "Do you know where this trail goes?"

The other lady replied in English, with what seemed to be a heavy German accent, "To zee vaterfall, zee beautiful vaterfall. Vater, zee source of all life."

I said, "Thank you," and kept climbing upwards, wondering if it was the same stream I had come across high above. Then it struck me that it was a strange thing to say, "Water, the source of all life." I thought about it more and something resonated with me. Since it was an unusual thing to say, it was sticking with me and her accent made it all the more curious for me. I decided this was definitely a waking dream. I now had two clues to go on regarding Lena's whereabouts. She was in a hut in a camp like the one I had seen in my dream, and there was a waterfall. It made sense that a camp would be near water, but a waterfall was a bonus, something more unusual.

I was sensing that "listening" was paying off, but my anxiety over Lena was still gripping me. Thoughts of her safety haunted me. Was she being fed? The longer she was gone, the more I missed her. I had feelings that, once I found her, I would not want to let her out of my sight again!

Proceeding onward I could hear the rushing water getting louder as I neared the cascading stream. The air was getting misty and I knew it was nearby. Rounding the corner, there it was, a small stream cascading at least one hundred feet down the side of the mountain wall. Much of the water was turning to mist before it could land on the cliff ledge below. As I had discovered above, the surrounding area was like a micro-climate supporting a dense growth of lush foliage clinging to the mountain-side cliff. Finding a smooth rock in an area sheltered by overhanging trees from the mist, I sat down for a rest. The sound of the falling water reminded me of the inner sound of running water, and I began to sing HU with the outer sound. Soon my eyes were closed, and I could hear my inner sound and the outer sound of the falling water blending together. I began to think about how wonderful this was, connecting with nature, and how everything is connected. It helped me take my attention off my pain and concern for Lena.

Chu-Tay's inner voice broke through my thoughts as he said, "*I would like to continue our earlier discussion about Divine Will.*"

"*Do you know that everything in the universe is composed of spiritual energy at its lowest common denominator? When you think about it, Jack, it makes sense that everything is Spirit. We are all part of the universe of God, or another way of putting it, is that we are all part of the "body" of God. We are all part of this infinite energy system yet we are all vibrating at our own unique wavelength which gives us our totally unique qualities.*

Harmony is actually a very real state. To live in harmony is to be in a state of compatible vibration with the "flow" of the universe, God, or Divine Will, and with those around us. It also means to be in a state of vibration that is complimentary to the rest of creation such as the animal, vegetation and mineral kingdoms that we coexist with.

There is a Divine Plan for all life and if we operate in harmony with the Divine Plan, our life and the lives of others, then everything around us will flourish and grow spiritually. Disharmony, on the other hand, is to operate from the viewpoint of the self. It means to ignore the whole of life and to be solely focused on needs we have created out of our mental concepts. It means that Divine Will, in the end will prevail, and so the shortest route to achieving anything is to move and work in har-

mony with Divine Will. To do this we plan with our minds, but we check with Divine Will."

As he spoke I could feel a lightness enter my being, a feeling of almost floating. I was tempted to open my eyes to see if I was, but I did not want to disturb the communication and the experience.

"We also work with all life by not imposing our will upon it. We live by the law of non-interference, another key Spiritual Principle. This includes not interfering with another person with uninvited advice. Harmony also means to have a minimum impact or disturbance on our natural setting. It starts with a respect for others and nature, for all life in fact. It is allowing other life to be as it is, and to manage its own life direction, not to create it for them.

Remember, Jack, not my will, but Thy will be done. You can ask God for advice anytime. When the mind says 'this way,' know that it is possible to bend; to accept that there is another way. When things are not flowing for us, it is a signal to stop and assess our situation. It is an opportunity to let go and open ourselves to Divine Will. My will or Thy will. Accepting Divine Will is living in harmony."

His words faded off and the sound of the waterfall brought me back to conscious awareness and the fact that I was getting wet in the mist. I stood up and headed back down the trail. I still needed more clues if I was going to be successful in finding Lena. When I thought about her, which seemed like all the time, I had a sweet, contented feeling mixed with apprehension for her safety. I could see the French-German hikers I had spoken to a long way ahead, as I climbed down to the base of the mountain, and it looked like they were taking pictures. There was still an hour of good light left in the afternoon as I caught up to them. I stopped to ask if they had been on this trail before and where the other end leads to.

The man responded in English with a very distinct British-French accent, "This is part of the Royal Inca Highway system was built long ago and leads past some other Inca ruins. It follows the Urubamba River past a power dam on the way to the next village."

"Power dam?" I questioned, my curiosity suddenly aroused.

"Yes", it gives life to the whole valley, and the ancient Incas even used the water there for power to run their grain mills."

Grateful for the information, I said, "Thank you, have a wonderful day," I continued on thinking that was a funny choice of words. There was that expression again. He had said, "It gives life". Maybe this was another clue, a power dam, and a waterfall. Now that would be significant, I thought!

I headed back down the trail for another forty minutes thinking about Chu-Tay's last words. He had said something like, "Let go and open to Divine Will."

When the light started to fall to shadows in the valley I was just reaching the town. I got a nudge to get some dinner in town for a change, so I walked along the main street following the railroad tracks, then turned up a narrow cobblestone side street. The shops were all still open and I looked into a few as I made my way along to a big square which opened up. There were three restaurants around the central plaza. After looking at their menus, I chose a seat outside on the patio of the first one I had looked at. The only thing I could think about was Lena and the clues I felt I had gathered. "What's next?" I thought.

Chapter 16
Life is a Spiritual Adventure

I ate a fresh pan-fried trout dinner on the patio in the main square of the town, which I would have enjoyed more had it not been for my concern over Lena.

Then I headed back up the mountain to the lodge. The sun was just slipping over the last mountain peak to the west, plunging the ancient city into dark shadows. The long climb and hike had tired me out, and I ended up in bed at eight o'clock.

August 21

I was up again before five a.m. and looked out my window. Some faint early light was beginning to creep into the still starlit sky. After showering and shaving, I got dressed in my hiking gear again, then sat down to do my spiritual exercise. I began to sing HU and placed my thoughts on seeing Lena having decided to ask Spirit for help in this contemplation exercise. I began to think of my love for Lena, feeling my heart opening to her. After what seemed to be about ten minutes, I had a strong feeling that Lena was ok at the moment. Then the word "Chacha" entered my consciousness. It was a strange word, like the Latin dance, the Cha-cha-cha, and I resolved to remember it. Ten minutes later, on coming back to physical awareness, I reached for my pen and wrote down the word, "Chacha" in my journal. Perhaps this was another clue, I thought.

I added a few other notes in my journal, then headed downstairs for an early breakfast. On passing the reception desk, I got an inner nudge to ask for a larger map of the region. I walked over to the clerk who was sitting behind the front desk, dozing.

"Good Morning," I said, and he jolted upright, somewhat embarrassed.

"Do you have a map?" I asked. "I have the map of the Machu Picchu area, but I would like to see a map of the region, if you have one."

He bent over and looked underneath the counter, then looked up and said, "We only have one map left. Let us have a look at it."

He pulled the map out and we opened it together on the counter, and he gave me an orientation of the Urubamba River and Agues Calientes. It was there that I spotted Chachabamba, just upstream from Aguas Calientes. There was the "chacha!" I pointed to it and asked, "How can I get to this town?"

"There are no roads along the valley, just the railroad," he replied, trying to stifle a yawn.

"Hydro electric dams?" I probed further.

He looked at me curiously and pointed out the two he knew of and said, "This supplies the power to the whole area. This place was also used by hikers years ago as an access point to the trail."

He ran his finger along the map pointing out the Inca Trail also called the Royal Inca Highway, the route the ancient Incas used to travel between towns in their empire. I folded up the map and offered him a few Peruvian soles coins which he accepted with a weak smile. I was feeling great, having collected the new clue, so I decided to defer breakfast till later and head straight up to see Chu-Tay. Another visit to the police station was also in order later this morning, I thought, to see if there was any news.

The walk up the trail in the dawning light was refreshing as I mulled over the information I had put together. Power dams, probably a waterfall, a hut in the woods, Chachabamba. It certainly made sense to me that kidnappers would be located in an isolated area, but with access to power.

Chu-Tay was inside as I approached the entrance to the hut. Greeting me with a grand smile, he asked, "How are you doing today, Jack?"

"I'm feeling better, now that I've collected some clues about where I may locate Lena."

He smiled a smile that gave me a new measure of confidence, as if to say I was on the right track. "Jack, sometimes it is best to go at a balanced pace so that you can catch the messages Spirit gives you. You have had some experience with this since we last met?"

"Yes, I replied with enthusiasm. I feel like I have been able to gather several clues yesterday and this morning." I continued to tell him about the waking dream I had talking to the hikers on the trail yesterday and about getting the word "Chacha" in my spiritual exercise and then looking at the map just before coming up here and discovering there was an isolated settlement up the river called Chachabamba.

He poured me out a cup of tea and handed it to me, which I thanked him for.

He smiled and replied:

"One of the best expressions of how to live your life is to live it as a spiritual adventure no matter how dark life seems. But what often stands in the way are very old habits. Jack, your old habits are deeply imbedded in your drive for success. The biggest challenge you have is not speeding up now that you have found the benefits of a slower pace. The challenge, you will discover, will constantly reemerge for you to deal with.

My eye lids were getting heavy as the strangely melodic sound of his voice registered with me.

Despite knowing the benefits and actually living the benefits of a slower, gentler pace, Spirit may send a set of circumstances to test you. And so it seems with all of our major life lessons, they keep coming back in different forms to test our learning. In this case, you have learned the benefits of slowing down, but have you really? One has to be careful, as challenging circumstances can alter your newly 'learned' behavior.

And so living life as a spiritual adventure is a great expression that lets one feel how they want to be all of the time. Jack, try to feel like you are on an adventure all of the time. Know this, Jack, that when you are on the edge of uncertainty, you are on the edge of creativity, spiritual creativity. This means that you have let go of your plans and you purposefully allow your life be uncertain. By doing this you are placing each moment in the hands of Spirit. You will be living moment to moment."

The edge of uncertainty. I thought, what a great concept!

Picking up on my thought, Chu-Tay continued, *"This edge of uncertainty is a creative state. It allows Spirit to direct us. We are allowing what we have set in motion to manifest in God's way. Thy will be done."*

Chu-Tay's voice turned into silence. Momentarily, I opened my eyes and Chu-Tay was still there! I had so many questions for him, but for some reason all I could do was sit there in silence and contemplate on his words. After a few minutes, I realized there was nothing more to say, that he was helping me in his own way, and I felt grateful, very grateful. I looked up and I thanked Chu-Tay for his advice, and slowly got up out of my crossed-legged position. He reached over and grabbed my hand, seeing that I was stiff and not used to sitting that way, and pulled me half way up, from his seated position.

"Learn from your quest, Jack," he said as I lifted the flap and moved through the door. I looked back into the hut to reply, but he was gone!

I headed back down the trail in the full morning sunrise and stopped half way down to the lodge to take my jacket off. "Learn from your quest," were his last words, I recalled. I wondered if he was telling me more than I realized on the surface? I remembered other phrases like, "Become more open to the way things unfold." I resolved to take my time and not to rush around, but to continue to be open to clues that Spirit was offering me.

I still managed to beat the crowd in the dining room for breakfast, then caught a bus down the mountain to Agues Calientes. I was thinking about

Chu-Tay's words, and in particular, his choice of the word "quest." Was he suggesting a quest, an adventure? Yes, I thought, he had also used the word "adventure." What could I do to create an adventure? Or was there more? Things to learn?

I walked up the now familiar main street with all of these thoughts roaming around in my mind, entered the police station and spoke to the duty officer. I gave him my name and asked if I could speak with the Commander. Nervously and expectantly I paced around the reception room and after several minutes he appeared. He greeted me in a pleasant but business-like manner, and my heart felt that if had he had good news, he would have been more up-beat. He led me to his office again where I sat down in front of his gray metal desk, now piled with stacks of files.

"Our national security office still has no new information but we have heard from Mr. Sandberg, through his company, and he will not be able to do anything until his return in two days to Sweden," he began. "He is in a remote area of Tibet, as we knew before, and transportation is difficult, they say. I'm afraid I don't have better news for you and your lady friend senor. As you can see, our national security people have sent me some files," as he gestured to the stacks on his desk. "This is a very serious matter, and we are going to do all that we can to make a successful resolution to the problem. Please be patient with the process, Senor."

"Gracias," I said in my limited Spanish. As I stood up and walked out of his office, I had a helpless sinking feeling in my stomach that there was nothing but bureaucracy helping Lena at the moment. I felt like they were applying textbook tactics to the problem. In that moment the full realization hit me—I knew that Lena's safe return was somehow up to me!

I left the police station and headed back down the main street to the bus terminus wondering what the next step would be. The sun was reaching down into the valley now and shining on the town's streets. As I passed one of the many hostels, a group of hikers was assembling outside on the walkway and I could see they were setting out on a long journey, judging from the size of their packs and equipment. On the side of one of the equipment bags was the logo, "Compania Camino Inca." Inca Trail Company, I thought. I got a sudden flash of insight: The trail runs right past Chachabamba. Then a second wave of insight hit me with a little chill of recognition: Chu-Tay had been talking about a quest. His last words were, "Learn from your quest."

An invisible hand seemed to lead me toward the steps and I was drawn into the lobby of the hostel like one magnet attracting another.

Chapter 17
Finding God

Inside the small lobby I looked around for anyone that looked like they were in charge, and I spotted a short thick-set man with a wide brimmed hat who appeared to be in his mid-thirties. He was organizing equipment and packs as I walked up to him and greeted him, "Buenos dias. Are you with the trekking company?"

He looked up and replied, "Si senor, I am Paulo, the guide. Can I help you?"
He stood up and shook my hand with a smile.

I smiled and asked, "Where are you going with this trek?"

"This is our standard four day trek along the Inca Trail," he said. "We take the train to Cusco and then connect with others and take a bus to the start of the Inca Trail at kilometer eighty-two. Then we trek back to Machu Picchu along the ancient highway. The trip takes four days."

I looked at my watch and the date. It was Wednesday and I was scheduled to leave on the return flight Saturday. In that moment, I realized it didn't matter. Everything could wait. Life had become a blur, one day rolling into the next since Lena had disappeared. My heart was telling me she was more important than anything else right now.

"Do you have space on this trip?" The words just popped out of my mouth without even thinking.

He looked at me and said, "Just one hour ago at our breakfast briefing we were full, but we have had a sickness and one couple has had to drop out. The train leaves in one hour."

"I would like to come," I said with an excited heart, " but my things are up at the lodge up top."

"You can make it, but you better run," Paulo called to me as I dashed out the door. "Meet us at the train station. You will see us."

I ran the three hundred yard dash to the bus terminus, caught up to a bus just pulling out and knocked on the door. The driver stopped abruptly, opening the door, and I jumped in before he could say anything. There was room for me in the back row of the bus as the other four squeezed over a little to let me sit. I introduced myself, and they turned out to be Canadians. I thanked them and told them that I was trying to catch the next train out of town back to Cusco for an impromptu trek on the trail.

As the bus neared the top of the run, I got up and moved to the front of the bus. As it pulled into the terminal area at the lodge, I could feel a few glares from some of the other passengers as I jumped off the bus first and ran to my room. I collected my hiking gear and stuffed it all into my day pack along with everything I thought I could use, then packed the rest in my suitcase. This really would be an adventure, I thought, as I ran down the stairs to the front desk. Luckily it was quiet and I was able to check out quickly and check my suitcase until my return.

The bus was empty on the way down, and I looked at my watch and saw I had fifteen minutes. I looked down into the valley and noticed that the train had arrived at the terminal. At the bottom, I jumped off the bus, swung my pack on and jogged up to the station past all the shops and restaurants to find the group loading the last of their equipment on the train. I found out later that the group would pick up the porters on the way, near the start of the trek, so they had to pitch in and load all the tents and cooking gear at the beginning.

Paulo was showing the tour party where to store things, and when he saw me, he came over and we confirmed the details of the trek. He signed an agreement for me and I signed his waiver as well endorsing one hundred and forty dollars in travelers checks. The train whistle blew, he grabbed me by the arm, and we jumped on board as the train started to roll out of the station. I handed him the signed travelers checks, and we shook hands, then he showed me a seat near the others. The train rolled up the main street and passed the Machu Picchu Pueblo Hotel with its red-tiled roofs, where I had first stayed in Agues Calientes, and then we were chugging out of town, following the banks of the Urubamba River.

I kept my eyes peeled for signs of power stations and waterfalls on the way. I was also looking for signs of Chachabamba, but at times the train tracks would leave the rim of the river's edge where the valley was wider, and in several sections, not much could be seen in the dense high-altitude tropical forest. After a few minutes, I got up from my seat and leaned over to Paulo, who was sitting across the aisle with a black haired woman, and asked, "Can you tell me about the town of Chachabamba? Is it just ahead?"

"Yes, he replied, Chachabamba is an ancient archeological site about three kilometers inland from the river. It is off the main trail, so very few people visit it. There is a small train station at the river, but you have to flag down the train

to get it to stop, otherwise it keeps on going. Mostly mountain farmers use that stop to get their crafts and produce to
the market in Agues Calientes and up river."

"Are there waterfalls or hydro electric stations in the
area?"

"Yes, I grew up in the area. They built the station when
I was a child. It is up in a mountain pass on the other side
of the Chachabamba site. Why would you want to know
this?" he questioned as he looked at me curiously.

"The receptionist at the lodge told me," I replied, trying
to avoid the question and my real reason for asking.

Just then, the lady beside Paulo grabbed his arm and
pointed out the window at several llamas being led by a
farmer wearing a round-brimmed straw hat and a red poncho alongside the railroad. We all leaned to look out the
window. The white and brown llamas were adorned with
colorful green, red and yellow ribbons in their ears and
looked very cute, and many on the train were desperately
trying to get their cameras out to get a shot before they
were too far away. I slowly sat down, grateful for the diversion and able to avoid another question from Paulo.

About ten minutes later we passed by the small wood
building that was the train stop at Chachabamba and continued on, winding through the valley. There was nothing
else to see and my heart sank a little. The trip was the same
timing as on the way up to Agues Calientes, four hours.
I spent most of the time staring out of the window in the
morning hours lost in thought, thinking about Lena and how
I could find her as we wound our way through the Urubamba valley towards Cusco. I thought about how she had held
me so tightly with her head on my shoulder in the ruins, after

Chu-Tay had spoken to us, when we had both had our visions of the past. We were together then, and I knew I had to do everything I could to be together again with her in this lifetime.

The white capped mountain peaks of the high Andes were etched against a clear blue sky and soared thousands of feet above, in sharp contrast to the lush tropical vegetation in the valley which was at about nine thousand feet in altitude. After another hour into the journey, I closed my eyes and began to drift off as I sang HU to myself. I did this out of habit whenever I wanted to relax. Soon I was gone, as the inner sound filled my hearing. I could feel Chu-Tay in my consciousness, and his words became clear as I focused on visualizing him.

"Your spiritual search for signs to find Lena is really about shifting consciousness: Soul's ultimate goal is God Consciousness. One way to think of God is as awareness or consciousness. In the human form we can only know God in this way.

We are also consciousness. We are a part of the essence of God, Spirit, and Spirit is what comprises us. We need to know this in order to begin our search for God, so to speak.

God is a consciousness of love. And so for us to know God we must identify the qualities of God. We then need to begin to adopt the qualities of God in our search to know and understand God. In effect, we learn about God by being God-like. We unfold by opening up to God's love and by then passing it on. This process is one of changing awareness. We have set ourselves upon a path of personal discovery at this point. This is the first step, to discover who we truly are. We are then able to continue our unfoldment as we continue to practice being more God-like.

God's main plan is for Soul to learn the qualities love, joy, compassion, humility, and service-to-others. We are knowing God by moving closer to God in our thoughts, words and deeds in harmony with these qualities. And so, consciousness is defined as our degree of awareness of God in how we operate our lives. It is our degree of acceptance of God in all things that we do, and living our lives in harmony with spiritual principles. We become something greater, and we become the living example of God.

This is how we come to know God. This is how we find God."

Chu-Tay's voice faded and I shifted into a wonderful reverie for an indeterminable time.

The train blew its whistle, jarring me awake. I opened my eyes and discovered we were just pulling into the station in Cusco. I had fallen asleep, half conscious of my inner journey for at least two hours. The sun was high in the sky, and it seemed that everyone on board was groggy. We got off the train and made our way to a parking lot where our bus was waiting for us. We were all handed a box and discovered this was lunch, so we all stood around eating our sandwiches and apples while the train station porters brought out our gear and stacked it near the bus. Then Paulo got us organized. We all pitched in and hoisted the gear up to the roof of the bus. Paulo was up top stacking it, then covered it with a tarp and tied it down. The driver arrived and we all stepped aboard the small bus for the ride to our starting point on the Inca Trail. The group was casually talking to one another, but was not really interacting yet.

We left the train station on the bus, and I counted fourteen in our group all together. We wound our way out of Cusco on narrow streets under blue skies. A half hour out of town, we stopped in a small village where Paulo had a pre-arranged meeting with a large number of porters. They were all very short and in traditional native dress with open sandals. After asking several questions to the men in a mixture of Quechua, the native language, and Spanish, he selected six of the local men as porters. They all took off together to buy food for the journey. The rest left, disappointed at not getting work.

We were able to explore some craft displays and have some tea in a roof garden café. Forty-five minutes later the porters were back. Paulo invited us all to board the bus, then the porters loaded our food supplies in the aisle of the bus. With the porters standing, we were on our way. The bus was jammed to over-capacity! I counted twenty-two seats and twenty-eight people on the bus with aisles filled and a full load on the roof top.

We wound our way through back-country roads in the highlands at over ten thousand feet, and passed some barren mountains. Other slopes were lush with green foliage and any that were not really steep were terraced for crops. For the last hour of the bus trip to the trailhead, our driver skillfully navigated what seemed to be a cow path where we met several vehicles, mostly other returning busses that had taken trekkers to the most popular starting point of the Inca Trail. On several occasions we had to stop or back up so both vehicles could pass.

We let the porters clear the huge load in the aisle and then we all jumped off the bus, eager for the start of our trek. Paulo handed us each our trail passes and then the park guard in the Warden's post stamped each one. After passing through the checkpoint, not unlike a national park gate at home in the States, we started out on the trail at around three in the afternoon. The porters were still back at the bus sorting out their personal loads and would be following us. We walked along a gentle inclined trail that seemed to follow the Urubamba River. Then the incline got steeper on the hard-packed rocky trail, worn with the footsteps of thousands, perhaps even millions over the centuries. The sun was brilliant and the surrounding mountainsides verdant. Alongside the trail were grasses and shrubs, and the air was a perfect seventy-two degrees.

Paulo had told us on the bus during our briefing that this would be an easy "training" afternoon, but as the incline got steadily steeper, I realized I was not used to carrying a full backpack in these conditions. I quickly found myself at the rear of the group. There were descending trail sections, as well, where I could pick up my pace a little, but on the whole, as we proceeded along, I gradually fell further and further behind until eventually I lost sight of the others. But I felt secure in the knowledge that the porters were behind me, as it had taken them longer to load the supplies and equipment on their backs.

However, to my chagrin, it did not take long for the porters, much smaller native area men, about five feet, five inches tall, to pass me as well. Amazingly, each was carrying up to thirty-seven kilos, about eighty pounds, the legal limit in Peru. The first two porters to pass were carrying all the tents, then one passed me carrying a large icebox, the refrigerator, and then others with the propane tanks. They were moving at an unbelievable pace and on the downward slopes were literally running in their open sandals!

We had started our trek at two thousand five hundred meters, about eighty-five hundred feet, and Paulo had said we would be trekking through two valleys before reaching our camp site. Overall, the terrain got progressively rougher and we were either going up, or down. Nothing was flat that afternoon. As we pressed on, the trail changed from hard-packed dirt with small rocks, to rough rocks from the size of basketballs up to three times the size of a watermelon. The longest climb began an hour before camp and it just about exhausted me. The only thing that kept me going was the thought of helping Lena and being ever alert for clues.

I stumbled into camp at dusk, the last to arrive by about two minutes. The porters had already set up the stove and were preparing refreshments. I discovered we were camped at a small farm by a mountain stream in a tiny community area called Hatunchach. I was exhausted, as we had climbed to over ten thousand two hundred and fifty feet, or three thousand meters altitude, an overall gain of seventeen hundred and fifty feet on the short afternoon trek. And this was just the warm up, the "training afternoon" as Paulo had called it! It seemed that my leisurely pace climbing Wayna Picchu in the previous days had done little to condition me for this.

The little farm consisted of a cooking hut made of hand-made clay bricks with a thatched roof, a sleeping hut, and an open shelter with just a thatched roof. There were a few chickens, llamas, and a green pet parrot. I sat down with the others in the open shelter as porters served us early evening tea, while other porters set up the tents. During the conversation at tea, I found out that the porters were incredibly strong and agile, and they had grown up doing this kind of work in the high altitude of the Andes. I thought of the little boy running down the mountain to entertain the tourists and could see how the local people could develop their stamina and strength from a young age.

After tea, Paulo led us up the hill and pointed out our assigned tents which the porters had set up. I stumbled to mine, rolled out my sleeping bag and lay down, totally exhausted. The night temperature of sixty degrees began to set in, a contrast to the daytime trekking temperatures of between sixty-eight and seventy-two degrees, depending on whether we were up or down, in sun or shade, or whether there was wind or calm, or any of the many combinations.

A half-hour later the bell clanged and I managed to make it up off my back for dinner. We were served a pasta soup starter, followed by very tasty whitefish, fries, and tomato and cucumber slices. I finally had a chance to meet and chat with the rest of the group. There were two college students from Wisconsin, who had arrived first in camp, a Canadian couple in their forties who obviously did a lot of hiking, a very sturdy older couple from Brazil in their late sixties, a couple from Bolivia in their early forties, three very strong younger men from Israel in their late twenties, who had just come out of the army, and a very social couple of newlyweds from the Netherlands, Lanny and Sonia. As experienced trekkers, Lanny and Sonia quickly sized up my difficulties with the trail and offered me some of their arnica cream. Lanny squeezed out a blob onto some tinfoil. He handed it to me and told me to rub it into my legs from top to bottom to help heal my leg muscles. I gratefully accepted the gift.

After thinking about the warm-up run and my performance, and being so sore, I resolved to speak to Paulo about getting a porter to carry my backpack.

After dinner I managed to corner Paulo for a minute. He said he would talk to the cook to see if there was any room in their load for an extra bag, but that there would be a cost. I also asked him to mark my map where we were, and to draw the trail route for me. Even though he was busy and very tired he spent a couple of minutes explaining the journey we were about to take, because I had missed the orientation at breakfast back at the hostel.

I headed up the hill a hundred feet from the house to my tent shortly after dinner and was able to get a look at the night sky, a brilliant blanket of stars, contrasted on all sides by the mountain peaks in black. It was absolutely beautiful. I then flopped into my tent, took off my pants and jacket and crawled into my sleeping bag.

I kept my flashlight on and took another look at the map for possible hydro electric installations. I could see four icons that looked like dams marked within reach of the trail. I needed more clues, I thought. I was really missing Lena. In a way, I felt like I had been robbed. We had just met and were getting to know each other, and then she was taken out of my life. I started to feel angry, but I knew in my heart that I should not go there. I would not find Lena if I promoted a "pity me party" in my head. I needed clarity and focus, to be tuned to Spirit. I knew that I needed to be outer-focused, not feeling sorry for myself, that I needed to stay positive and without fear. I was discovering that when my thoughts became fearful, it felt like my inner awareness was turned off. And I definitely needed my inner connection to solve this challenge and find Lena.

152

As I lay there thinking about her and trying to remain positive and open to the inner guidance, Chu-Tay's words from my dream-like reverie on the train, which seemed like yesterday, played in my head. I remembered his words, *"This process is one of changing awareness."*

Sleep came almost instantly after that last thought.

Chapter 18
Understanding Consciousness

Paulo had said the night before at dinner that we would be using the light to our maximum advantage for the trek, that we would be up before dawn, and we'd be on the trail at day break. Fortunately, I was naturally an early riser. So when I heard the porters preparing breakfast before any light in the sky, I was feeling better. At least here was one area in which I was more conditioned than the others. Paulo was one of the most experienced trek guides in Peru. He had told us at dinner the night before that his ancestors were descended directly from the Incas. Of his entire family lineage, only his father had any outside blood as his he was of half-Spanish decent. Paulo told us he had grown up in the remote region of Madre de Dios near Manu in the jungle region to the east of the Andes and had personally explored all of the ancient ruins in the Urubamba River valley region, also known as the Sacred Valley.

As I lay there awake, I thought to myself that Paulo, if anyone, would be able to tell me about any hydro electric dams in the area. It was still dark, but the sky was beginning to get a little gray, so I decided to do my spiritual exercise still lying in my sleeping bag. I was soon aware of the inner sound and a gentle golden light filling my inner vision. Chu-Tay entered my consciousness and I could see him smiling a reassuring smile and I sensed he was telling me that I was doing well following the inner nudges. I had felt some doubts after the long journey on the train and bus yesterday, but I now perceived that the adventure and the risks were not only to help Lena, they were also for my own spiritual development. Chu-Tay's words began to flow through and register in my consciousness.

"Jack, you are a being that, as Soul, is gaining in consciousness. We are conscious of our basic needs when we are born and as we grow into our teen years, we begin to define ourselves. At this stage we become very self-absorbed. Some people never progress beyond this state of self-centeredness. But there are other stages of growth that are possible for us characterized by more caring, more giving. In fact this stage of our development is where we can begin to consciously see our relationship with and discover our true nature as Soul.

The discovery of who we are is a process of unfoldment. It is a dedicated process to reach out to others like you are now reaching out to Lena, and in the process we are able to reach inward to discover more about ourselves. This lifetime is about rising above the basic nature of man and becoming something greater; more open, loving and forgiving. This is the gift we have been offered.

Our true vocation is as a server of life, to be a co-worker with the Creator. This is our goal as Soul whether we realize it or not. In summary, consciousness is characterized by the amount of love you can accept from God and also the love you give as it has been given to you."

The next thing I was aware of was the soft bird whistle of a porter, his creative way of rousing us as dawn was about to break. I stretched, then crawled out of my sleeping bag and put on my pants and jacket in the chilly air. I packed the rest of my gear in my pack and left it by the tent. Walking down the hill, I shivered a little, joining the others for breakfast and a briefing for the day. Half of the porters were cooking and serving breakfast, the others breaking down the rest of the camp.

When we were all together, Paulo advised us that we would climb most of the day over the highest pass on the trail going from ten thousand two hundred and fifty feet above sea level, or three thousand meters, to fourteen thousand, three hundred and fifty feet, about four thousand, two hundred meters. After Paulo finished, I immediately walked over and spoke to him about having my pack carried by a porter, and he gave me the good news. There was room in the cook's load for my backpack for twenty dollars, which would be paid directly to the head cook. I gladly agreed on the spot! In retrospect, I believe this was the best twenty dollars I have ever spent! Ever!

Fortunately the arnica cream had done its magic overnight, and my legs were feeling quite good. As day was just breaking, we departed camp and climbed steadily, following a valley. The trail turned into a steep staircase of rough rocks as we ascended the mountain beside a roaring stream. In less than a couple of hours, we were all sweating in the brilliant sun, but as we proceeded vertically alongside the stream we began to enter a cloud forest that gave us dense shade. Paulo called a break, and I sat down to make some notes. My hand was shaking from the fatigue already, just a couple of hours into the five hour climb. All of the trees were covered in moss and vines, and the tree trunks were very smooth and almost wet to the touch. After the short break we were back on our feet.

As I climbed steadily with the others, I was silent most of the way, lost in thought and looking for clues to help me find Lena. Proceeding still upward, our trail pulled about fifty feet away from the cascading stream and we broke out above the cloud forest, once again under blue sky and brilliant sun. The snowy peaks jutted against the sky as we continued up the Inca staircase to the half-way point of the climb to the pass. Here the trail moved completely away from the stream valley we were following, and the temperature rose as we left the moist air from the stream behind. I was delighted that I was able to stay with the group, albeit the others were carrying their own packs.

At a strategic rest point, we came upon colorfully dressed female Quechua natives, the wives of local high-altitude farmers who were selling bottled water and energy bars. Some of our party took advantage of the treats. Paulo told us these would be the last local farmers we would see on the trek as we proceeded into the more remote region the Royal Inca Highway followed. The mountains were now a mix of green foliage and rock. We climbed to the end of the large valley which would end at the pass, the highest point on the Inca Trail at over fourteen thousand, three hundred feet.

Now the steepness of the surrounding mountain slopes was too great for even the llamas and alpacas. As we plodded onward and upward on the narrow trail, I could feel the air become much thinner about an hour away from the top of the pass. Then the trail incline became so steep that the trail turned into another never-ending rock staircase. I could only ascend sixty steps at a time before sitting down to catch my breath on one of the numerous rocks that bordered the trail. Many of the others were doing the same. As I stepped up, I would quietly count to sixty to give myself a goal for each set of steps, before stopping to give my heart and lungs time to recover. As we got closer to the top of the pass, more and more of the snowy peaks of the high Andes were visible.

I began to think about patience and about slowing down during the last half hour of the ascent. After all, I thought, there was no hurry, as I could only now manage a few steps before stopping to fill my lungs with the thin air. I thought, "the agony and the ecstasy"—gasping for air and then stopping for a minute until my breathing returned to "normal" at fourteen thousand feet. I had plenty of time to drink in the snowy mountains and the valleys in numerous shades of green to green-brown.

I came to a life-changing awareness on that last part of the climb. I observed that most of us would move at a quick pace up the steps and then stop to rest while a few of our group would move very slowly, but they would have no need to stop and rest. They would just continue at their slow and steady pace. The older Brazilian man was one of these slow and steady pacers. As I sat there catching my breath on a number of occasions, he would slowly walk by, one step at a time. He would get about twenty steps ahead of me, but then I would get going and pass him. But as I stopped to rest, he would pass me again. He always arrived at the summit of every climb at the same time, but he was never exhausted. He enjoyed every moment, every step of the journey while I enjoyed the resting, but considered some of the climb an agony. I thought to myself, life should be more like the tortoise than the hare, and in that reflective moment of insight I resolved to slow down and enjoy every moment of the trek.

At about one-thirty in the afternoon I reached the top of Huarmi Wanusca, meaning "Dead Woman's Pass" in English, and got a round of applause from the others that were already resting there. As the rest of our group arrived, those who had arrived earlier gave each a genuine congratulatory round of applause which lifted everybody's spirits. I stood there taking in the incredible three hundred and sixty degree panoramic mountain pass view; snowy peaks of the other mountain ranges as a backdrop, and the trail winding up the valley we had just ascended. Then I flopped down on the mountainside just below the top to keep out of the strong chilly wind funneling through the pass. I recalled Chu-Tay's words, "learn from the quest."

The half hour break came too soon, and Paulo got us up off our back-sides. We were off, heading down the other side of the mountain pass, also a rough stone path with steps in the steep sections, which constituted most of the trail. The view on this side of the pass was equally spectacular as we descended the other side of the mountain. By late afternoon we reached our campsite beside a roaring mountain stream. I was low on water after such a long climb, so I immediately walked over to the edge of the stream and filled my water bottle adding a purification tablet.

The porters had beaten us by at least a half hour, so they already had the tents pitched and tea on the stove for our arrival. Too tired for tea, I found my tent and crawled in. I took a minute to rub some leftover arnica cream on my thighs and calves. Exhausted at four in the afternoon, I felt grateful for the porter carrying my pack. I lay there listening to the roar of the stream—thirty feet away—for three hours, but I managed to get myself up for dinner at seven o'clock.

Paulo explained during dinner that our location was called Pacaymayu. He went on to tell us that there were originally twenty-four thousand miles of Inca Highway stretching from Ecuador in the North to Chile and Argentina in the South. Every twenty-four miles there was a rest station, not unlike our interstate highway rest-stops today. Cusco was the center, the hub, and all roads led to Cusco, the "Rome" of the region.

After speaking to the group, Paulo came over to me and quietly said, "I could hear you last night in your tent. I was checking the site, and I could hear you singing HU. I also sing the HU." I was delighted. I smiled and said, "I have been singing the HU for a few years now. When did you hear about it?"

"It has been a tradition in our family for many generations," he said, "but we have had to be very quiet about the HU. There has been much persecution in the past for those that disobey the church."

I thought to myself, here is a potential friend I could trust, and in an instant I got an inner feeling to share my mission and reason for my last- minute decision to join the trek with him.

Paulo was listening to my every word as I explained how I had met Lena, how Chu-Tay was giving me guidance, and how I had followed my intuition and trusted the waking dreams I had noticed so far. He had given me several nods of understanding, like he knew exactly what I was talking about.

He said, putting his hand on my shoulder, "My friend, I think I can help with your mission. I have seen some unusual activity in an area off the trail on the last trek."

"Where is this area?" I asked.

"We will come near it by night-fall tomorrow," he replied. "Let's talk more after dinner."

My heart was racing. I thanked him for his support, and we finished getting dinner ready. I thought about trust; about trusting others and also trusting my inner awareness, my dreams, intuition and waking dreams.

Chapter 19
Life Cycles

Lena was in my thoughts over dinner and I was wishing I had a photo of her to look at. After dinner, I moved off to sit on a rock with a vantage point to survey the almost magical scene of the valley below. The sun was sinking on the horizon and only the snow-capped peaks were lit now with an orange-peach glow. I could see Paulo approaching me now, and my heart beat with anticipation.

"My friend," he said in a low voice, "I have been thinking about your clues, and I have a possible location. I have seen some unusual activity in the Urubamba valley, and there is a power dam there at a waterfall. It is an ancient site of the Incas, but it not easy to get there. The main access is by an old trail. No one but a llama could get from the bottom of the valley to this trail way up here but there may be a way."

I began to share some of my other spiritual experiences with Paulo, and he shared some of his including what he called Soul Travel. He told me about his contemplations, visualizing places he wanted to visit or see and that the experiences often became like vivid dreams which he could remember clearly. As we chatted and shared our realizations and experiences, I could feel a strong bond of friendship growing between Paulo and myself.

After about an hour, we were both tiring and Paulo offered, "I am going to Soul Travel to the power dam and waterfall tonight and we will talk in the morning. Let's get some sleep."

We said goodnight, and I headed over to my tent. I was excited about what he had said, but I was even more curious about what he'd said about Soul Travel. I had never heard of it. I was in bed by eight-thirty as the stars were beginning to pop out in the crystal clear night sky. I could hear the squeals and screams of the brave ones taking showers in the wash-up hut, located beside the glacial stream and by the sounds of it, there was a direct pipeline from the stream to the shower heads.

Laying there, I sang HU to spiritualize my dreams, and I was asleep in seconds.

August 23

I awoke before dawn with the vivid recollection of a dream. In the dream, Paulo and I were swimming in a small lake together. I tried to think of what the dream could mean, and I thought to myself, water usually means Spirit to me, and we were both in the water together. Maybe the dream was telling me that Paulo was with me spiritually? I also got the strong feeling from the dream that he could help find Lena.

I lay there and began to sing HU silently to myself, because I didn't want to wake the others. We were all in our tents and the porters had pitched them close to one another on the only area of relatively flat ground in the area. I was quickly deep in contemplation when Chu-Tay's words began to enter my consciousness.

"Jack, everything in the universe or the worlds of God has an ebb and a flow. We are all part of this ebb and flow of life. Just like the tides, we can see the rush of change enter our lives, and you can feel this now.

The cycles of change are in constant motion and it is up to us how we view our lives. We can choose to recognize these natural changes and live our lives with this awareness, or we can resist the cycles, which can be very difficult for us.

Pain is a great teacher: It usually means resistance to something, a change, or perhaps an attitude or belief or an emotion we hold that is no longer valid for us. The cycles continue and so do we until we reach the end of our long cycle, this lifetime of learning. One of the greatest secrets to having a great life is understanding this flow of change, and to constantly search for ways to grow with it."

His voice trailed off with the last words, and I wondered if my life was somehow connected to Paulo. The porters brought me completely back to being awake with their gentle bird calls. I zipped out of my sleeping bag, put on my pants and crawled out of the tiny tent. Looking at my watch, I could see it was six o'clock. I got my pack together and left it by my tent for the porters as agreed, headed over to the cooking tent and joined several of the others.

After a delicious breakfast of scrambled eggs, bacon, bread and coffee, we set out in the cool morning air as the sun was progressively lighting more of the sky. We climbed steadily upward for forty-five minutes to an ancient highway stop, some wonderfully preserved ruins called Runcu Raccay, a round, now roofless stone building, reaching it before eight o'clock. As I climbed up yet another seemingly endless ancient Inca staircase to reach the site, it seemed like a metaphor for life, full of steps. Some are very steep and difficult, I thought, and often we just have to go slowly, while others are downhill, a time for acceleration and accomplishment. And there are flat sections -very few on the Inca trail—that seem like the rest points of life. I mused that the Inca trail was a perfect metaphor for what Chu-Tay had said.

At the site inside Runcu Raccay, Paulo gave us a briefing and explained that the building was thought to have been a tambo, a kind of way post for couriers following the trail to Machu Picchu, as it contained sleeping areas for the couriers and stabling facilities for their animals. We then left and continued our climb upward.

At nine o'clock we reached a second pass at thirteen thousand, five hundred feet. Paulo gathered us around him at the summit and explained there was a tradition on the trail, to honor it by placing a stone on a cairn. Paulo picked up a small stone and placed it on top of a couple of rocks on a rock outcrop. We all followed Paulo's lead, including the porters, by finding a stone and placing it on his. We created a small cairn of our own, and I silently gave thanks to my legs and the arnica cream from Lanny and Sonia, and to God for the many blessings that had come my way in the last few days.

The sun was hot but with a cool breeze, the temperature was a perfect seventy degrees for trekking as we continued onward. After an hour and a half, we stopped at another ruin called Sayac Marca, a well preserved Inca Town built on a promontory of rock, overlooking the trail and effectively controlling it. Paulo led us up the narrow, steep steps, which were very treacherous, but the only means of entry into the structure. When I got up to the top, I was startled when screams broke out. As I turned around, I saw a man falling down off the narrow, crooked old steps. He landed about ten feet down on a narrow ledge and rolled over toward the cliff, but he was stopped by the size of his back pack from rolling further, just two feet from the edge of a cliff that, from my vantage point looked virtually bottomless! We had found a group of trekkers at the archeological site and he turned out to be their trail guide named Mario. A few moments later, I could hear the excited members of his group calling him Super Mario as he was being pulled up off the ledge, shaken but not harmed.

Paulo led us to a great vista point in the ruins and explained that Sayac Marca means dominant town. Sayac Marca had a hydraulic channel to supply water to the town with three Inca fountains. He pointed out that there were several temples as well. It was believed to have been a stopping place for pilgrims where they purified themselves before reaching Machu Picchu, the sacred city.

Leaving Sayac Marca, we trekked down a long rock staircase through a beautiful cloud forest of dense lush subtropical foliage, past a waterfall and through an amazingly beautiful canopy of trees, vines and moss. We were well above the clouds hovering in the valley, as we looked down over the edge of the footpath. The trail actually hugged the cliff in this section. As I moved along over the large rough rocks that "paved" the trail I was followed by the chirping of melodious crickets. I noticed the appearance of beautiful yellow and purple flowers, cactus, and bushes with orange flowers alongside our ancient route.

For the first time I was not last to arrive for lunch. But I was also still the only one not carrying a pack. I was grateful to Paulo for suggesting that I buy a walking stick from one of the local Quechua entrepreneurs we passed on the first morning. It was a blessing to have in order to navigate the half-mile long staircases that made up much of the very old Inca highway system in the jagged terrain.

Our cook, Carlos, served us a beautiful vegetable soup followed by fish and noodles and a choice of coca leaf tea, anise or black tea. After a half-hour nap lying on the grasses in the searing high-altitude sun, we continued as the trail now hugged the rim of the mountain, which had been walled up in numerous places. As we pressed on, clouds rolled up the valley, and we found ourselves walking in a refreshing mist and light rain. Further along on the trail, we descended through an antediluvian highway tunnel about seventy-five feet long. The Incas had carved it right out of the rock where the mountain side was too steep for a trail along the edge.

Around mid-afternoon as we arrived at another Inca site, Phuyu Pata Marca, meaning city above the clouds. We actually did break through the clouds as we reached the higher elevation of the site and in the brilliant sun we were offered a spectacular view. The site contained six fountains and a long chain of ritual baths fed by a spring higher up, and was believed to be another purification point for those traveling to Machu Picchu. Paulo explained that the high-est bath was reserved for the nobles, while the lower classes performed their ritual ablutions in the waters of the lower baths.

The trail out of Phuyu Pata Marca spiraled and de-scended steeply towards Huinay Huayna, another Inca ru-ins which Paulo translated as "Forever Young." We plodded down what seemed to be another never-ending staircase, what I could only describe as treacherous in many places. The mountains at this point were green and appeared purple in the late afternoon mist around three-twenty. We continued to descend the stairs which followed the fall line of the mountain for an hour. Then the narrow pathway began to hug the curve of the mountain, and we climbed down a mix of steep rocks and stairs for another two hours, which made our hiking sticks positively indispensable.

I arrived in camp at five-thirty, absolutely drained after the ten hour trek but feeling like I was getting stronger and recovering faster. Our camp was located in Wina Wayna where there was a trekkers lodge and washroom facilities. My tent was pitched on a terrace, just three feet from the edge of a cliff like many of the others. Paulo gave us a quick briefing on the evening's schedule and then set about on his own to explore the area. He was gone for about twenty minutes and then returned and waved for me to come over.

"Come with me. I have something to show you." He led me across a ridge, like a bridge over a crevasse, where we could look straight down into the valley and the river below. He pulled out of his pocket a tiny pair of binoculars and handed them to me. Pointing to the north, he said, "What do you see?"

I took a look and spied a waterfall with a small cement building beside it and some transmission lines. A little ways downstream I could see a hut and some tents. My heart skipped a beat—it looked just like I had seen in my inner vision!

"This is the place!" I exclaimed. "But how do we get down there? It seems impossible."

"I was Soul Traveling last night," Paulo whispered, "and I saw the primitive pathway I explored as a child. Although

I was not sure when you told me about your vision, my Soul Travel confirmed my feeling. If you are full of adventure, we can go down and take a look tonight under the full moon while the others sleep."

I was amazed and could not wait to get started, even though I was exhausted at the moment. I was also getting very curious about Soul Traveling as well, and I was trying to form the question in my mind for him, but he was already crossing back over the stone bridge to get some dinner. As I turned to follow him I replied enthusiastically, "Yes, let's do it!"

Chapter 20
Mastering Change

As we ate dinner, Paulo explained to the rest that he and I were going to do some exploring, and that we would report back in about an hour or so. Paulo and I left the group, and I followed him along the edge of the cliff-like slope at the top of the valley for about a hundred yards. Then Paulo turned and said, "Let's sing HU and do some Soul Traveling together to spiritualize our mission. We can turn our exploration over to Spirit and place the outcome in God's hands. I am going to ask to be shown what we need to see."

I was delighted with his suggestion. I felt that we had much in common and that he could teach me a lot about applying spiritual principles in solving challenges in everyday life. I thought of what Lena might be going through and felt a pang of worry. We sat down cross-legged beside each other on the rocky ground facing down the steep slope, and closed our eyes. I asked silently for guidance and to be shown what lay in the valley or for a sign of reassurance. Paulo started to sing HU, and I joined him. After what felt like a couple of minutes I began to feel lighter. I started to hear the sound of rushing water and I began to see sparkling light, like the sun glistening on water. As I followed the inner experience I felt as if I was in the light and was being bathed by it—then a scene opened before my eyes. I was standing in a waterfall looking out on a river. The vision lasted for what seemed to be about ten seconds and the scene faded and I could hear Paulo's voice say "Baraka bashad." These were the same words that Chu-Tay had said to me on several occasions!

I opened my eyes and Paulo was smiling. "You were there too?" he asked.

"I was in a waterfall, looking out down the river!" I said with a quiver in my voice, I was so excited.

He picked up on my excitement. "Yes, I had the same vision. Now I know that we can go there from here!" he exclaimed. "You can Soul Travel too!"

I was amazed to learn that I could ask for help and be shown a location or visit a destination, to see from the Soul perspective. Paulo was already up, and I scrambled to get up and follow him along the edge of the valley. We went another hundred yards, then Paulo stopped and said, pointing down into the valley, "There is an ancient pathway down there towards Chachabamba. This was a sacred site of the Incas, and the waterfall was the place of many rituals of purification. The site is connected to the Royal Inca Highway by a hidden entrance, and I believe we have just both traveled there in our Soul bodies."

He turned to continue, and I spotted something in the rocks and scrub brush that looked like a step. "Paulo, what's this?" I called, and he turned around and looked. He smiled at me and then took a step, and then pushing aside more brush, took another one. In a matter of seconds we were taking large steps down the side of the valley that were hewn out of the sides of the steep slope. We descended the archaic staircase, partially hidden with overgrowth, for about half an hour as the shadows were creeping into the valley. The valley floor was mostly in shadow when we stopped at the bottom of the staircase. We were now about one hundred feet above the river and could hear the waterfall. We looked around and could see no indication of where the path led as the area was covered with thick scrub brush.

Paulo decided to head toward the sound, and I chuckled to myself that we were "following the sound" of rushing water, one of the sounds that I heard so often in my spiritual exercises. I thought, *I wonder if we will be guided by the light too?* No sooner had I thought the words than I saw a glint of sunlight. It was the setting sun casting a last ray on the waterfall at the top. I pointed to Paulo and we headed straight for the glistening light as well. We arrived near the top of the waterfall where a small mountain stream was gushing from the side of the mountain and down to the other river that powered the hydro electric facility. The stream was flowing out of the mountain, and I could feel my energy connecting with this place. In fact, it actually felt sacred, I thought after a few moments. I was uplifted by the light-energy feeling the waterfall was creating, and the prospect of finding Lena.

Paulo looked around and motioned me to come over. He had discovered a narrow crevice, about four feet wide, and a step. He jumped down and soon we were slowly ascending another rough rock-strewn staircase, this time into a black abyss. It was getting very dark and very damp a dozen steps down, so we stopped to adjust our eyes to the light, and then continued descending. The steps were as steep as a ladder, so it was slow going in the murkiness down the damp, slippery staircase. Paulo found the bottom and guided me down the last three steps.

Standing there in the void, I could hear the roar of the waterfall. Paulo led me forward as we felt our way along a narrow crack in the rocks, and I knew he was testing each step before putting his weight down. The sound got progressively louder. I could feel the air getting very moist, and then upon edging around a corner, the passage got a little lighter. We found ourselves standing on a narrow ledge behind the waterfall. We had done it! My heart was pounding with the excitement of possibly discovering Lena's whereabouts.

It was too dark to see through the falls as I had done in my Soul Travel experience. Paulo turned and shouted over the roar, "Let's come back tomorrow when the light is better." My heart sank, and I fought the idea for a moment. Then realizing he was right, even though I was anxious to press on, I followed him back. We slowly retraced our steps behind the waterfall, to the steep steps, then up and out of the fissure in the rock. It was almost dark as we started up the staircased trail to camp.

It was one of the most challenging climbs I had ever made, up the giant rock staircase, after the day's trek on the trail and especially feeling so close to Lena and having to turn back. I had to stop numerous times to catch my breath and rest my burning legs. Back at camp, Paulo gathered the group for a briefing and told them about our adventure. We then headed for our tents. I was so tired I could hardly get my pants off. When I did, I found the arnica cream I'd been keeping in the piece of foil and rubbed it into my leg muscles. I zipped up my sleeping bag, and I remember singing HU three times. In my half waking, half sleeping state, I became aware of Chu-Tay's face. He was beginning to speak to me inwardly, as always, in his richly intoned voice.

"Jack, it is important for you to understand that Soul needs to grow and therefore will have the experience or lessons it needs; It needs to work through the challenges that are a part of its destiny. Soul is therefore attracted or 'magnetized' to

certain experiences, people, and things that will produce the experiences it needs. In other words, we are drawn to these experiences for our growth as Soul. For example, you have been searching for Lena because you have this powerful feeling of love. You miss her dearly. You feel very connected when you are together?

I silently agreed.

Because Soul wants to grow, this simple fact is the cause of change. Now we do have our choices, because change does not have to be a rough experience. One key to reducing the impact of change is to be in tune with Soul's urges to grow. This means to be in tune with our inner nudges and our inner knowingness. Soul does tell us when it is time to do something. However we often ignore the nudge, because we are comfortable where we are, or we do not trust our inner voice. So accepting big change is often a challenge. One needs to give themselves time to change in-between.

Jack, look forward to your adventure. I will be with you inwardly to help you through the undoubted changes that will be a part of your life. Keep a true focus with your spiritual exercises and be a strength for others to maintain this dedication and pursuit of your growth. Who knows, perhaps you will have someone who understands this as well, to be with and share many of the same challenges, but in their own unique way."

His words drifted off and I fell into a deep sleep wondering if he meant Lena.

Chapter 21
Taking Responsibility

I woke up before dawn. I knew it was still black out as I could not see a thing in the tent. I reached my hand out over my head to test the temperature, and it was chilly, but I also noticed that my hand did not touch the tent wall. I groped for my flashlight that I had placed near my head and turned it on and discovered that my sleeping bag had slid down some and that I was hanging about a foot outside of the tent. Wiggling a few times to pull myself back inside, I reached down and felt the bag. It was damp but not wet, thank heavens. Then I remembered where we were situated. Our tents were pitched only about four feet from the cliff-edge, the only area where the porters could position our tents, which happened to be somewhat sloped. I had crawled into bed at an incline with my head uppermost and I had slid down in the night.

I remembered the others coming back to their tents after I had gone to bed. They had wakened me up a little as they were stepping over the ropes of my tent, catching their feet in the dark as they walked along to get to their beds. A flashlight was a mandatory piece of equipment here, and I had wondered at the time in my half-sleep if we would lose any of our group over the edge.

Now awake and breathing in the chilly morning air, I lay in my sleeping bag to do my morning Spiritual exercise. I began quietly singing HU as usual and Chu-Tay appeared quickly. Each time lately, I had been noticing that it was taking less and less time to attain an inner awareness and connection. Chu-Tay appeared in his hut in my inner vision, and I realized I was actually Soul Traveling. I could see everything very clearly and I was really there, yet I knew my physical body was somewhere else high in the mountains camped on a cliff-edge by the Inca Trail. He invited me to sit as usual, and poured me a cup of tea, which I accepted.

He looked at me across the fire and began to speak:

"The old saying, 'What comes around, goes around' is an expression of the Principle of Cause and Effect that you are probably familiar with, Jack. You will eventually receive back that which you give out. If you give out love and good cheer to all, that is what you will receive back in your life. Conversely, if you hurt or interfere with others, that too will return to you.

So, taking responsibility for our behavior in this life and also for what we set in motion in our previous incarnations or past lives as Soul springs from the Principle of Cause and Effect. This Principle is very exacting. There is no ducking the responsibility we must accept for our every action, thought, and word. As we understand this Principle better, the lessons come back to us more quickly. In other words, karma speeds up and the time lag between our action and the result it creates becomes shorter. We can then begin to see cause and effect more easily. This helps us to recognize that this Principle is indeed in operation and teaches us the importance of changing behaviors that are no longer serving our need to advance as Soul.

As we move into a greater awareness of this Principle and take responsibility for our circumstances, we empower ourselves to move forward and make changes in our attitudes, behaviors and our relationship with others. Then we begin to understand what the journey is all about."

The vision faded, and I began to come back to the awareness of the hard ground pressing into my bones and the gentle sounds of the wake-up bird calls of the porters. The grumbling voices of the others could be heard as they too struggled to get up off the hard ground and tried to locate their flashlights to get dressed for the day. I unzipped my sleeping bag, reached for my pants beside my head, got them on and crawled out. I had been in the habit of sleeping in my T-shirt, socks and underwear due to the chilly temperatures at night in the high Andes.

I sat in the dim morning light and tied on my boots. Turning on my flashlight, I could see the tent lines clearly and followed several others along the thin pathway near the ledge just a couple of feet from the cliff. We climbed over the other tent lines and then headed up a steep, narrow trail. We joined several others at the dining tent who were sitting around quietly, still groggy from sleeping on the hard ground and the hard trekking we had done the day before.

When everyone arrived, Paulo gathered everyone around for the day's briefing. He began, "Buenos dias! I wish to tell you I have a plan that will require us to stay in this camp for part of the morning." There were a few friendly groans and grumbles about staying in bed or going back to bed.

Paulo laughed and continued, "Last night I told you about the trail Jack and I explored. I believe it was for a reason that we were led to this place. There is a woman we believe we can help down there, a friend of Jack's, and I would like to ask the group if you would be willing to stay an extra few hours so that we can help her?" The group turned to one another looking bewildered. Paulo continued, "It will be an opportunity for you to watch the sunrise and enjoy the wonderful scenery here and perhaps even catch up with your journal notes or take some photos." Most nodded their approvals knowing how much they would be able to enjoy the rest. Lanny said, "I don't know about you guys, but I'm going back to bed after breakfast!"

"You may have an extra hour. I will tell the porters to take down the tents last, but they will have to get everything ready, and they will leave before we do, so everything will be set up at our next camp when we arrive," Paulo advised. "Jack and I will then be leaving as soon as we have finished breakfast. We are going to climb down into the valley and see if we can locate her."

"One other thing," Paulo added, "I will ask the porters to give each of you some energy bars and fruit for your packs, and be sure to fill your water bottles up for the trek and add your purification tablets. The water is very clear up here but there is still bacteria."

Paulo and I grabbed our flashlights and some rope, and he put some food into a backpack. We set out along the rim and edge of the valley as the dawn was breaking. Carefully we made our way back down the overgrown staircase, and the light almost seemed to illuminate our way as the sun rose in the sky. We easily found the crevice in the daylight at the place where the waterfall sprang from the mountain side, and we climbed down into it after tying our rope to a large rock at the top. This would make the descent into the crevice and the return climb out a lot easier than the last time. We reached the bottom and edged our way along inside the damp passage as the roar of the waterfall got louder and louder. Soon we were standing behind the waterfall, bathed in the mist and the roaring sound of the pounding water. Paulo motioned to me to move over to a spot where the waterfall was just a light mist and we were able to see out and down the stream. There was a hut. And about a hundred yards beyond it were some tents. As we stood there we saw a man carrying a tray with what looked like plates of food up to the cabin. He disappeared inside and then came out about fifteen seconds later.

I shouted in Paulo's ear, "What do you make of that?"

He pointed and said "Lena's probably in there!"

I nodded my agreement. The camp was awake and we could see about a dozen men in view milling around their tents and there was a truck in a clearing. It looked like they were camped in order to guard the site from the other direction. The railroad passed by that side of the site some distance away near the river. Our end of the ravine was probably a dead end. It certainly seemed that way from our trail down the primitive staircase that had fallen out of use.

Surveying our location in the morning light, we could see that the waterfall spilled into a pond at its base, and we could easily swim under the falls from our position to the bank. Near the cabin the pond narrowed and flowed down the valley like any mountain stream. We watched for a while, and after about fifteen minutes the man returned, entered the cabin and then left with the tray and dishes. I had a strong urge that *now is the time!* They won't have to come back until lunch, I thought.

I motioned to Paulo. He nodded, and I knew he was getting the same feeling. He turned to me and yelled, "Let's check it out!" He peeled off his backpack and set it on the ledge, and I took off my jacket. Then we both sat down and took off our boots and socks. I knew my clothes would dry quickly as I had bought quick-drying adventure pants and shirts, knowing there were frequent rains in tropical areas, so I left them on. I stepped forward into the falls and then slipped into the pool. I wanted to scream but caught my breath instead. The water was positively glacial! Paulo was next to me, as we came up together on the other side of the pounding water. He frowned a frigid look and motioned to the shore of the pond. The whirling current was strong but not as powerful as I thought it would be. I swam a few careful strokes, then reached down with my foot and discovered I could touch bottom. I looked at Paulo beside me and got a strong deja-vu, a kind of chill of recognition. At that moment I remembered the dream from the night before last. This is what I'd seen!

I got a surge of confidence from that inner connection. I pushed off toward shore keeping only my eyes above the water, lifting up to breathe through my nose in order to stay as low as possible. We were both swimming the breast stroke to be as unobtrusive as possible and to avoid splashing. As we reached the shallow edge, we crawled flat on our bellies and elbows to the edge of the bank where the pond narrowed into a river, and pulled ourselves out. We lay flat on our backs in some scrub and brush, catching our breath. I peered out to be sure that we were not seen. Then after a minute, we turned over and crawled to some tall brush, about ten feet away, toward the cabin.

Paulo rose to look through the grass and had a clear view down to the tents. He could easily see the men, but none were in our vicinity. He motioned to me and we crawled another thirty feet so that we could approach the cabin from the back without being seen by the men. Paulo whispered, "We'll have to make a run for it," indicating the clearing around the cabin. I nodded in agreement, and we both broke into a crouched run toward the back of the hut. Reaching the side of the cabin, we stopped to catch our breath and listen for any sign of the guards. All was quiet, and I slipped up to the rear window, raised myself up and looked in.

The window was filthy, and it was dark inside. I could see nothing for a minute but as my eyes adjusted, I could make out a bed and someone on it. My heart started to pound. I could see blond hair tied back into a pony tail, and I recognized her jacket. It was Lena! I was shaking, I was so excited. Through the dusty window pane I could now see her feet and hands tied to the bed. She was just as I had seen her in my spiritual exercise a few days ago!

I slid back down and motioned to Paulo to look. He peered into the window with his hands cupped around his eyes to block out the light, making it easier to see inside. He looked back at me and reached into his pocket, smiled, and pulled out a knife. I whispered, "We don't have much time. They'll probably be back soon to check on her."

Chapter 22
Spiritual Relationships

I sang a silent HU to myself, remembering to pause and take it slowly; I peeked around the corner of the cabin. Nobody was in sight, so I quickly moved across the front of the cabin, opened the door, and slid in with Paulo right behind me. Lena looked up and was just about to speak, but I held my finger to my lips to stay quiet. She caught herself as I dashed to her side. She appeared tired and looked like she had not been able to wash for days. Paulo cut the ropes, and she lunged into my arms crying. I held her for what seemed like an eternal moment. It reminded me when we held each other tightly in the building at Machu Picchu as she was sobbing on my shoulder. Our present danger brought me back to the task at hand, and I got a hold of her arms and pulled her back, whispering, "We need to go—right away!"

She looked at me with tears of joy and said, "Thank you for coming for me, Jack. I have been thinking about you all the time since they took me here."

"Me too," I whispered in her ear. "It's been quite a journey."

"I think there are guards all around. How will we get away?" She asked shaking.

"Trust me, we have a way," I reassured her. "Follow Paulo, my friend. We have a secret way out. But first, let's get your shoes on. Leave your pack"

Paulo was already at the door and opened it a crack and waved us over. He crouched out around the corner of the hut and we were right behind. I was last, and gently closed the door behind us. We crouched as we ran up to the taller undergrowth, and then we crawled through the brush, returning the same way we had come, up to the edge of the pond close to where it narrowed into the river. I motioned to Lena to stay low and to follow Paulo, crawling into the water keeping as low as possible. Lena hesitated as Paulo crawled forward, but I gave her a gentle push and whispered aloud, "The passage is behind the waterfall." She looked at me with an incredulous expression, and quickly crawled and slid into the icy water with us, shoes and all, now that she understood our route. There was no time to try to keep them dry. She followed Paulo's lead, doing the breast stroke once our feet could no longer touch bottom. We swam across the now swirling water, the mist providing us with some camouflage as we neared the falls. Lena stopped to look at me as if to say, where are we going? I pointed ahead as Paulo disappeared under the pounding water.

She followed, took a breath and ducked under the water with me close behind. Paulo grabbed Lena's arm and pulled her head up and she came to a stop right beside the ledge just past the falling water. Paulo hoisted himself up and then pulled her up behind him while I gave her a boost from behind, and then I hoisted myself up as well. We stood there shivering in temporary safety on the ledge behind the falls, and we all looked through the falling water to see if we had been noticed. There were a few men milling about by the tents, but none were near the cabin, so it looked like our visit had not been discovered.

Paulo and I put on our packs, socks and boots, and then Paulo led the way back through the blackness of the narrow passage, illuminating it with his flashlight. He flicked it off after we rounded the corner, as the sunlight spilled down through the crevice allowing us to see. We proceeded up the rough stairs in the crevice with the aid of the rope we had tied at the top, and when we were out I pulled the rope up behind us. Carefully we made our way, crouching through the chaparral to the bottom of the trail steps which led to the top and our camp.

We began our ascent up the mountain staircase, and were about a quarter of the way up the steps when a shot rang out! A bullet hit the wall about ten feet ahead of me! We all crouched down and Paulo got his binoculars out to see.

"There are two gunmen down there!" he exclaimed. "Lay flat for a minute so they can't see us."

Lena and I were flat on the steps in a second as another shot rang out. A bullet had hit the wall just beneath me.

I shouted to Paulo, "I wonder if they know how we got up here?"

"It won't take them long to find out," he said. We must have left some clues with the flattened brush and water on the floor of the hut. We don't have much time to lose."

After a brief pause, he continued, "Now I feel badly that I didn't send the others on ahead with the porters!"

He took a peak over the edge, and then yelled, "Let's go!"

We ran crouching up the steps and more bullets rang out, but they were way off their mark. Within a few seconds I realized that we were out of range, as the bullets were hitting the wall below us. And then the steep mountain wall turned and we were out of sight. We all stopped to catch our breath, we were so winded, gasping for air. After a minute, Paulo got us going again, and we climbed up the seemingly never-ending staircase, an ancient part of the Inca highway system. My legs were burning with each step but I pressed on, full of adrenaline, helping Lena as much as possible.

We arrived back at camp in the mid-morning sun, exhausted and cold from our mission. We found the others scattered about taking pictures, making notes in their journals, and just hanging around. Paulo shouted to everybody to gather around. The rest of the group scurried over quickly and asked if the noises they had heard was gunfire.

We were standing there with our clothes still wet to damp as Paulo began to speak as he caught his breath: "Everyone, this is Lena. We found her in a cabin in a very unhappy state, and we were able to free her." There was a round of applause from the group with comments of "fantastic" and "excellent."

Paulo confirmed their suspicions about the gun shots. He continued, "There are some bad guys that are now very unhappy and they may try to follow us. We have no time to lose, so I would like to get us on the trail in five minutes."

Panic and fear was evident on their faces as Paulo, speaking in an extra calm voice asked, "When did the porters leave?"

Lanny piped up, "About an hour ago."

"Good. Who can loan Lena some dry clothes?"

"I will," offered Betty from Canada, "She's about my size."

"Wonderful," Paulo exclaimed. "Let's do it! Be ready to pull out in five."

Paulo immediately changed into dry some clothes, but the porters had my pack. It didn't matter anyway, because my clothing was drying quickly in the morning sun, and the temperature was in the high sixties already. With all of the climbing, I was actually quite warm.

A few minutes later we were moving across the valley ridge as fast as the group could travel with back packs. I tried to give Lena some idea of how I was able to find her between breaths, but she seemed confused by all that I was telling her about waking dreams, deja-vu moments, Soul Travel, and subtle messages from Chu-Tay, mixed in with the events of what the police had said and meeting Paulo. When we stopped, I would have to start from the beginning and give her the full story, I thought to myself.

We pressed onward, following Paulo until we could go no further. Lena and I were stumbling with exhaustion after the climb up from the waterfall and now with the fast pace of our trek. Paulo could hear us agonizing and about ten minutes later, he called a halt to the group near a little trickle coming out from the side of the mountain. "Let's sit down for a quick lunch," he said. "Everybody help yourself to your bars and apples and top off your water bottles. There is a little spring here just off the path for you. Remember to use your water tablets, though."

Resting was heaven as we sat on a rock together, contemplating all that had happened so quickly. I put my arm around Lena and told her I would give her the whole story from the beginning when we stopped for dinner.

She looked at me and said, "I wish I had a toothbrush. I haven't been able to brush my teeth for a week."

I laughed and said, "I'm just glad you're in one piece." I gave her a long hug. Then I pulled back a little, giving her a kiss on the cheek. It felt so good having her in my arms again, I had tears in my eyes.

Just then Paulo got us up off our comfortable rock seats after the ten minute break, and we headed upward following the now rocky trail through a beautiful alpine meadow, then skirting a craggy mountain peak. The trail then descended, making it easier on our legs and breath as we pressed onward. The views were spectacular as we trekked along, but somehow I was not into the scenery at this point, still concerned about the kidnappers and worrying if they were able to follow us. At one point we started to climb upwards again and I could see steps leading into the rock face. Paulo turned around and said, "We are entering another old tunnel. Watch your step!"

As we climbed up the steps I could see the passageway carved out of the rock in places, and in other places it appeared to be a natural formation. About a hundred feet ahead in the darkness I could easily see the exit and more stairs leading up the mountain. Many in the group stopped briefly to grab a picture of this unique feature of the Royal Inca Highway.

As the sun slid low in the West, we found the porters in a secluded rock outcrop, an ideal campsite where there was flat ground for the tents and where our camp fire and lights would be out of site from anyone coming along the trail. Lena and I collapsed on a rock from exhaustion. The others were feeling the pace of the day as well, but were keyed up with the new sense of danger that had been infused into the trek, even though we had not seen any signs of pursuit. I began to share with Lena my side of the adventure. A half hour later I'd told her about all of my experiences that had led me to her, including the reassurance I got humming the Beetles song, *The Long and Winding Road* and the words, "leads me to your door."

I was anxious to hear her story, but as I finished mine, Paulo called the group and the porters into the mess tent before dinner for a full briefing. He told them how he and I had found the ancient Inca staircase down to the crevice and then how we had found the passage behind the waterfall. They all sat spellbound with worried looks as he told of the rest of our adventure and the daring rescue. Bringing the group into the present moment, he explained, "We are at least one hour ahead of them if they find the passage under the waterfall. However, they will not be able to follow in the dark. This trail is too treacherous at night, so we can relax until dawn," he told the group.

The tents were all pitched. I found mine and showed Lena her new luxury accommodations. She looked in at the tent and the single sleeping bag and smiled and whispered in my ear, "I guess that will keep us warm if we also share our body heat."

"I don't think we have a choice," I replied faking an apology. Then jokingly continued, "I could always take you back to the hut if you prefer?"

She just looked at me and playfully stuck out her tongue at me.

"That reminds me, I have a toothbrush you can borrow after dinner!"

"Better from you than borrowing from one of the porters," she quipped.
I was delighted she had found her sense of humor again.

After soup, chicken, and pasta for dinner, Lena and I headed for our tent. I found my toiletries sac and pulled out my toothbrush and toothpaste, handing it to her. "You are a lifesaver," she said as she grabbed her water bottle and headed behind the tent. I chuckled at her play on words. After what seemed to be five minutes she returned to me and said, "I think there are still some bristles left," with a smile to show off her polished white teeth.

I took my turn, then returned to find her snuggled in the bag. I got my boots off and she unzipped the bag for me, so I crawled in. We were in each other's arms, feeling snug as bugs in a rug, happy to be together again.

It was about eight o'clock, and we were both ready for sleep. I decided I would wait for her to tell me about her experience when she was ready. We gave each other a long kiss and then she rolled over in the tight bag so we could sleep like spoons to share maximum body heat. Shortly after, I drifted off with my face buried in her hair. My last thoughts were about what Chu-Tay had said about karma and about my vision while with him and Lena at the ruins—about how Lena had saved me in that lifetime as a child. I realized that I was returning the favor, and saving her several centuries later.

August 25

I was awake before dawn and nudged Lena to stir her awake. I whispered in her ear to ask if she would like to do a spiritual exercise and she nodded. We both started to whisper HU, and as we began, I thanked Spirit for bringing Lena back into my life. We continued singing silently to ourselves and I became conscious of the two of us inwardly sitting in Chu-Tay's hut as he began to speak:

"You may sense already that your relationship with each other is different than others you have each experienced before in this lifetime. It is a reflection of your spiritual growth. You both have discovered that you need a new kind of freedom to be your true self—a new kind of space. This is reflected in the desire to share time with each other, but not every moment. So you each enjoy time to do your own things without having to offer an explanation out of guilt to the other. This includes having your own friends too. It is important to feel complete as individuals, meaning, you will not need each other but you will enjoy each other. You both have gained the awareness to not lean on the other for anything because you now take responsibility for your life and are content with who you are.

This kind of relationship that you have earned is essentially built on trust and communication. One first must have trust in oneself. This comes from an inner knowingness that life puts us in the right situation every time for our growth. And so we trust our inner being first. We trust our nudges and feelings, and we openly communicate and share these if we feel like we should. So we trust the process of life and this allows us to just be. As I've said before, Thy Will Be Done.

Your new relationship built upon a spiritual foundation is like two full glasses of water that stand side by side, each complete in themselves. Your previous relationships were more analogous to two half-full glasses of water, each needing the other to make a whole. There is a big difference. The former calls for genuine respect for the other and a complete trust. It also means being able to let the other go on a permanent basis if this is what they wish. You two have reached that consciousness where you are able to give each other new levels of trust and respect for each other's journey.

The next time we meet I will take you both to a special place. May the blessings be."

With that, Chu-Tay disappeared and I became aware of Lena rolling over to face me. She began kissing me, and I responded and experienced a feeling of peace and purity that I have never felt before. We were so close our noses were rubbing. I opened my eyes and saw that hers were open too, and in that moment I saw her love. I looked deeply into her big blue eyes and returned the feeling. I knew then that she had been there with me in Chu-Tay's hut.

"I love what he said about trust and communication," she whispered. All I could do was kiss her again, I was so enraptured with emotion.

We held each other for a few more minutes before his parting words started to register with me.

"I wonder what he means by a special place?" I asked. "Me too," Lena replied.

Chapter 23
Patience

As we explored the depths of each other's eyes, Lena said softly, "I knew you would come for me. When I was tied up in the hut, I remembered the dream I had. Remember the one I told you about when you rescued me? I just knew that it would come true, because it felt so real. It's what kept me going when I began to have feelings about ever making it out alive."

I nodded and gave her another kiss.

"Now we're even," I said. "Remember, you saved me in ancient Machu Picchu as a child."

Lena beamed a big smile, and just then I felt a hand on my foot. "Time to get up," the voice whispered. "Sounds can carry for miles in this valley," he said. "Be very quiet." It was Paulo. He was waking everyone up one at a time, not wanting to make any noise.

The sky was showing its first light as Lena and I crawled out of the tent. I gathered up my things silently, knowing we would be off to a very quick start after breakfast. I loaned Lena my comb and stood there for a moment looking at her, studying her features. I realized how beautiful she was, even though she was not wearing makeup. In fact she glowed with an inner beauty, I suddenly realized. That was it, I could see her inner beauty, and it was a new feeling for me.

As the last of the group entered the cook tent for breakfast, Paulo got us all seated and began to tell everyone, in a voice just above a whisper, of the dream he had in the night. "I dreamed that we were being followed, but that we had given the kidnappers the slip by taking a different trail."

He went on to explain that upon waking he felt he could remember a minor trail; a little known route out of the mountains, connecting to a campsite at Puente Ruinas. It was at the foot of Machu Picchu near the Inca Trail. He explained that this trail offered spectacular views but was not used these days, because it was longer and most treks were scheduled for four days. He asked if everyone was all right with trying to find the route and extending the trek by an extra day. After a few exchanges between couples, everyone agreed in whispers feeling that the unique trail and extra day was a bonus and would add some extra insurance to our safety. I realized that my return flight was yesterday, but by now, it was the furthest thing from my mind and didn't matter!

We quickly ate some eggs, cereal, bread and coffee, and got underway, a little ahead of the porters still breaking down the camp. They would easily catch us since they moved significantly faster once they were packed up, even with their seventy-five pound loads. Paulo said, "The old route will be difficult to spot. It has not been used much in recent years so it could be overgrown, but there are certain features to look for like steps, smooth table rocks, and cairns that were sometimes used as markers."

We all could feel the pressure of the possibility that the outlaws could be following us. Within a half hour the porters had caught up with us, but today they were staying with our group, helping to scout out the alternate trail. They were happy because Paulo had promised them a good bonus, twenty dollars each for the extra day's work—I had told Paulo I would gladly cover the extra $120. After about an hour we reached a high point at the top of a pass, and Paulo asked us to stop while he looked down the high altitude valley with his binoculars.

"Oh no. There they are!" he called out, not trying to cause alarm as he pointed back. "There are three of them." I followed his finger and I could see three men the size of tiny ants following about an hour or so behind. "We must press on as quickly as we can," he commanded.

I had just sat down with my arm around Lena and could feel her start to tremble. "I was so frightened," she whispered. "They were very rough. They put a bag over my head and were yelling at me in Spanish, and I didn't know what they were saying." I squeezed her tightly as she began to cry.

"Don't worry. Paulo knows this country. We will be able to hide," I affirmed trying to offer her some comfort, not knowing what else to say.

Paulo was standing up and began to lead us along the trail. I pulled Lena up in my arms to go, but something caught my eye off to the left. It was a little pile of rocks, too neat for nature to have created. I shouted, "Hey Paulo, look at that!" as I pointed over to the tiny cairn. We both walked over to look and he smiled. "This is it! This makes sense. Look, there's a step in the brush. Looks like our trail! We are at the top of a minor divide here, and all land falls to the North or South-West from here. This trail will take us to Puente Ruinas which is in that direction. We must be careful to not to leave any clues of our change in direction."

Paulo scattered the stones making up the cairn and then led us down the overgrown trail. We were soon out of sight of the high point of the divide from where we had spotted our pursuers where we had made the ninety degree turn on the pathway. Paulo did an excellent job of spotting the old route and moved us steadily downhill until we finally reached a lower elevation where vegetation was growing thickly. The air was getting warmer, and everyone took the opportunity to open their jacket. An hour or so later we were beginning to enter taller vegetation as the landscape became greener, and temperatures rose due to our descent in morning sun. By late morning, our jackets had to come off and it became clear that we were descending a long valley with a cloud forest ahead and below that we'd be entering. If the gunmen were following, they would have a hard time seeing us there, I thought.

In half an hour we were in the orchid clad tangle of the cloud forest, following a mountain stream cascading down the mountainside in a series of waterfalls. The trail was mostly overgrown, and we had to pull the branches apart in several sections in order to continue. The lush and tangled vegetation here was constantly shrouded in mist from the cascading water which created a typical microclimate. As we continued, the trail then veered left of the stream and began to turn upward again. For the next two hours, we continued over the naturally camouflaged trail as it snaked its way down and up over three more moderate passes along this ancient and remarkable route. In many areas this trail, like the main trail we had taken, followed ancient steps over very steep inclines, but the added challenge was that these steps were barely passable in sections due to the vegetation that had overgrown them.

Paulo was still leading and sighted Machu Picchu in the distance from our vantage point. He let up for a moment, and pointed it out for us at the end of the valley, about a mile ahead on the saddle between the two mountains. The view was truly magical, and Paulo decided it was time to relax for a half hour lunch break. While the porters set up the stove, made tea and prepared some pasta, I was able to find a quiet place with Lena and took in the view of the mountains with the ancient city in the distance. We closed our eyes and did a quiet HU for just a moment, and then I had an opportunity to make a few journal notes. Lena was quiet for most of the lunch, and then she conveyed to me in a voice filled with emotion, "Jack, I want to tell you all about my kidnapping. I need to get it out, otherwise I can feel the fear trapped inside me. Tonight, OK?" she questioned.

"I'm here for you," I replied. "I want to hear all about it when you're ready. I know it has been very difficult for you; terrifying I'm sure." We hugged a long hug, and I could feel her relax a little, knowing we were going to talk about it when we got to Puente Ruinas.

After our short lunch stop, we proceeded steadily downward into the valley and lost site of the ancient city, skirting it about a thousand feet below. By late-afternoon we arrived at the final part of the trail that seemed to end above the camp area, located in a valley gorge below. As I was wondering how we would be able to get down into the camp, Paulo asked us spread out to look for the way down. After about ten minutes, Sonia hollered and we all gathered around. There in the brush, she was pointing out a spectacularly steep stone staircase, similar to the one that led us down in the crevice behind the waterfall. As the sun ducked behind the mountains, casting long shadows in late afternoon, Paulo took the lead, and one by one we helped each other down the overgrown rock steps. Within about five minutes we were at the bottom and came out of the trees and brush outside of the camp, surprising some little children playing. We followed Paulo into Puente Ruinas which looked more like a farm with camp facilities.

Paulo entered the camp office and asked the supervisor for the use of a telephone to call the police while the rest of us milled around outside. Upon completing his phone call, Paulo told us the police officer would advise his commanding officer, but that the best place for us would be to stay in the camp for the night, and that the police would be here as soon as possible to interview us and make their reports. The camp supervisor said that the camp was very full, but that there was a small bunk house where we could sleep considering our circumstances. He led us over to the cabin, and our porters pitched their cooking tent. The rest of us laid out our bags on the sets of double-width bunks that were three high. Lena and I flopped down on a lower bed for a much needed rest, and I could feel her relax more, knowing that the police were on the way, but too tired at the moment to talk.

Our porters put together dinner consisting of soup, vegetable patties, and tea. It was delicious and we ate until we were stuffed. Then I suggested to Lena we walk around the camp before it got completely dark, hoping she would talk about her ordeal. It wasn't long before she began to speak: "Jack, I want to tell you what happened," she said with her voice shaking.

She looked into my eyes and I whispered, "I'm ready. I want to hear what happened"

"I was in the market in the afternoon, and all I could think about was meeting you for dinner. I wanted to wear something really pretty, and I was exploring the stalls and shops when I spotted a beautiful poncho hanging up high. It was purple, and the lady said it was made of baby alpaca wool. It was so soft and vibrant, so I asked if I could try it on. The lady went into her store to get a rod with a hook on the end to lift the poncho down. It was then that I felt a knife in my ribs. Someone gripped my arm so tight I thought it was going to fall off. The knife dug into my back, and I moved with him down the alley. He opened a door and pushed me in. It was dark, and someone inside grabbed me from behind and then put a bag over my head. It smelled like grain, and I could hardly breathe with the dust in the bag. I could see nothing. They pushed me down into a chair and tied my hands and feet to it and shoved a filthy rag in my mouth. Then I heard a door shut and I was alone.

"Several hours later I was really hungry, and I heard the door open. A voice in Spanish said something, and I was untied and dragged up off the chair. My hands were tied together in front of me, and then I felt a knife in my back and I moved forward. "Silencio," the voice said. I discovered that my hands were tied to a rope and someone was pulling me along. I remember I was tripping over things as they kept the bag over my head, and then I knew that we were outside when I felt the cooler air on my arms and legs. I was led by two or three men that didn't say much, but at times they would grab my arm and lead me over steps or rocks. Many times I tripped and almost fell.

"It felt like I was dragged all night along a trail, or whatever. Then I could hear the voices of other men that sounded excited. They were happy. I was led to the cabin and thrown on the bed. My arms and legs were tied to the bed, and then one or two of then left. Then the bag was ripped off my head and the rag taken out of my mouth, and one man was there. I could see that it was daylight. He said, 'You stay heere weeth us till wee get monee.' Then he smiled at me and left.

"The same man brought me food on a tray in the morning and in the evening each day and would untie one hand so I could eat. He would leave and then return in ten minutes to collect the tray and tie up my free arm again. When I would have to go to the bathroom, he would put the bag over my head and tie it around my neck. Then he would untie me and take me outside, and he would lead me about twenty steps away, then put some paper in my hand and say, 'Vamos.' It was horrible!

I lost track of the days. I had nothing else to do but think and sing HU. I had several spiritual exercises where Chu-Tay came to me. I remember him speaking of having an experience that I needed for my growth and accepting responsibility. And he also spoke about God's love, surrender and Divine Will and he spoke about Divine help."

As Lena told me this, I thought to myself that it seemed that I had received similar messages from Chu-Tay. Lena slowly continued, "Then several days later after breakfast, you showed up with Paulo. I must admit I was starting to despair, and I even had thoughts about flirting with the man bringing me the food to see if he would help me. I'm glad you came when you did, Jack. I'm so grateful...." Her voice was lost in her sobs as she cried on my shoulder for a few minutes. I could not say anything. I felt I should simply hold her and make her feel loved. When she looked up and I looked into her eyes, I said to her, "It was love that brought me to you. I love you Lena." And she kissed me with tears of joy running down her cheeks, and I kissed her back with tears welling up in my eyes as well. We were both trembling with emotion. We just stood there hugging each other in the middle of the camp. I could feel the release in her, and I sensed that we would both feel a lot better now—her having let out the experience, and me feeling it with her as she told me.

Eventually we slowly turned around and headed back to the cabin. It was dark inside and we discovered that several of the others were in bed. We quietly peeled off our pants and shirts and crawled into the double bed, a small luxury after sleeping on the cold rocky ground on the Inca Trail. Lena and I went straight to sleep in each other's arms after the long arduous day trekking and her sharing her terrifying emotion-filled experience. The remarkable experience was taking its toll on the two of us, and I was ready at this point for this adventure to end!

We were both able to start our sleep with a silent HU so as not to disturb the others. As I was just about to fall asleep, Chu-Tay appeared in my inner vision. I joined him inwardly in his hut with Lena in a vivid dream-like scene. And then he took both of our hands and led us out of the hut. We appeared to be floating upward, and I had a feeling of excitement and lightness as we moved into what I can only describe as another dimension. Soon we were approaching a great temple which seemed to glow of its own accord. The shape was that of a large domed structure with high columns leading up to the door, reminiscent of the architectural style of the Taj Mahal, and it seemed to be clad in gold!

A maroon-robed asian-looking man with a bald head and a strong golden glow about him smiled in greeting to us as he opened the door. We entered and Chu-Tay led us to the center of a great hall. The light inside was an intense pure white light which emanated from the walls and a single podium was positioned in the center. As I looked up I could see a shaft of golden light stream down from the center of the domed roof casting a dazzling glow about the podium. When we were led closer, I noticed a book on the podium. Chu-Tay motioned for us to sit on the floor, and he began to speak softly.

"Welcome to this golden wisdom temple. It is open to all who are spiritually ready to accept the ancient wisdom that is offered here. I would like to tell you about a challenging subject for me in my earlier incarnations—patience. This is a challenge that I had needed to work on for some time. In those early lifetimes before I achieved a degree of Mastership, I used to be a very frustrated person. Always frustrated about not getting what I thought I should receive, or seeing things happen on my schedule or in my way. It took me many lifetimes to determine the source of my frustration. I discovered then that frustration is very close to anger—that it is actually another form of anger, perhaps a milder form. I reached a point in my personal development in one lifetime where I felt I needed to have some answers, and so I began to take this constant frustration into contemplation, into my spiritual exercises.

What came to me was that I had to slow down. I was moving too fast. My life at that time was a constant process of getting somewhere, and I was always pressuring myself about never being where I wanted to be, when I wanted to be there. I definitely needed an attitude adjustment about how I was going through life—too fast and too often feeling resistance.

Through a series of spiritual messages in that lifetime, I was able to slow the pace by degrees. This was the beginning of my discovery about patience. I began to see that life was to be savored *and that one should 'see and smell the roses'. Of course, this allows us to move at a gentler pace and to go with the flow. My discovery was that I was imposing my will on the whole of my world, not an uncommon way for many people to go through life today. After all, we grow up being taught to think our way through life, to strive for what we want.*

As his words impressed upon my consciousness, a tiny pinpoint of blue light appeared in my inner vision and then grew into a tiny brilliantly radiating star.

The most productive way to go through life, I have discovered, is to feel our way. That is, to tune in to how things feel. To work with the heart or the gut in the sense of making choices. This is actually a very creative approach to living because it calls for a reliance on the higher self, Soul. Soul actually has the last word so to speak, so why not consult Soul in the first place? Patience is essential to catching the inner nudges and feelings.

I found in that lifetime the secret to being joyful is letting go. To create a plan, to set it in motion, but to let the outcome manifest according to Divine will. This applies to the smallest of plans like the timing of a dinner out or when one meets with friends. So build flexibility into your lives and allow plans to unfold in their own way. This was the most important awakening for me in bringing contentment into my life. The frustration disappeared, the impatience that caused it left, and I began doing the best I could to let my plans unfold in a flex-

ible fashion. This, I know, was a turning point in my earthly lifetimes after many incarnations with this challenge.

So what is patience? It is moving with the flow of life and being open to how our actions and plans manifest. Have patience my friends and life will serve you well."

I laid there thinking of his message while the blue star gradually faded from my inner vision.

As I fell into a deep sleep, curiosity about the temple and its location occupied my last thoughts.

Chapter 24
Spiritual Freedom

<u>August 26</u>

I sat bolt upright in bed, hitting my head on the bunk above with the sound of a loud voice in my ear. "Jack, Jack. Wake up! Wake up! You must leave right now. There are bandits everywhere." It was Paulo. We could hear the sound of footsteps in the center of camp.

"I think they have found us, or we have been betrayed," Paulo said. "They were able to follow us, or maybe the policeman tipped them off. You don't have much time. I'll stall them if I can or create a diversion."

Paulo left the room, and I was in a daze, trying to pull my senses together. It was pitch black in the room, and I had no idea what time it was, only that it was the middle of the night. Lena was awake and started to shake. I gave her a hug and said, "Let's get out of here!"

I reached for my flashlight and flicked it on as the others started to grumble and stir wondering what was going on. We hurriedly pulled on our pants, shirts and boots, and I grabbed my knapsack. Luckily there were some energy bars and our jackets in there with the rest of my stuff and I tossed my flashlight inside. We slid out of the cabin, crouching, and headed toward the back of it. I had a hold of Lena's hand as we dashed from shadow to shadow behind the other buildings at the back of the camp in the pitch black. It sounded like more men were arriving, and I could hear sounds of loud voices as the kidnappers began to question the other groups of campers in their tents and cabins. The only place where I felt we could go was back to the stone staircase that we had come down, hidden in the bush at the edge of the camp. Flashlights were moving about everywhere, and there were angry shouts and screams from terrified campers.

Moving quietly through the brush, I pulled Lena with my hand, keeping our profiles low. We found the location of the ancient steps in the dim moonlight, and step-by-step we slowly picked our way up the very steep staircase, afraid to turn on the flashlight. The sounds began to fade as we got further away, and twenty minutes later we reached the top where we stopped to rest and catch our breath. We could see down to the camp and watched eight to ten flashlights searching the tents, cabins and brush around the campground looking everywhere for us. It would not be long before they widened their search, I thought. I motioned to Lena that we should keep going, and we proceeded up the dark moonlit but barely visible, steep trail holding hands.

When the sounds below finally faded away I was able to relax a little. I knew Lena was terrified, and I wanted to take her mind off of our rude awakening and the bandits. I slowed us up a little so we could catch our breath as the incline of the trail lessened and said haltingly between deep gasps for air, "I had the most amazing inner journey——last night with Chu-Tay.——- You were there too.——Do you remember?"

"Yes," she said, breathing heavily from the strenuous climb and the adrenaline rush, "it was a very special place, just as he promised. It was beautiful, like nothing I have ever seen before!"

I could feel her grip relax slightly on my hand as we shared our spiritual experience from just a few hours ago. I looked behind, and there were no flashlights following us, so I slowed our pace even more, and we relaxed into a regular trekking rhythm. We silently climbed up the trail until the first light of dawn and then sat down for a rest on a large rock. As we caught our breath, Lena turned to me and suggested, "Jack, I'd like to just chill here for a minute and settle down. Can we sing a few HU's together? I know it will help me relax, emotionally."

In my anxiety, I looked sideways at her as her platinum hair caught the dawning light and a chill ran through my body! It was a chill of recognition, of being in this moment before. I was having a déjà-vu experience and a feeling of calmness washed over me. The experience was brief but enough to help me see that she was right. We needed to relax, even if it was just for a few moments. I knew that we needed to keep our balance and not react from fear. I felt that the only way were would survive would be to be in attunement with Chu-Tay and our higher wisdom. Insight and creativity were what we needed at this point. We had already done all we could do to distance ourselves from the kidnappers.

I said, "No signs of anyone following us. Let's do it!"

We were standing on the trail, still holding hands as we closed our eyes. As we began to sing softly, I watched my breath settle down into an easy resting rhythm. Soon an inner sound entered my awareness and Chu-Tay appeared. We were back in the temple, sitting cross-legged on the floor. The walls were glowing with a pure golden-white luminescence and there was a sparkling golden light shaft illuminating the book on the podium in the center of the hall, the golden wisdom temple as Chu-Tay had called it.

"What is this place?" I asked inwardly.

"You are in the temple of Gare-Hira in the Spiritual city of Agam Des which is hidden in the Hindu Kush Mountains. You have been welcomed here in your Soul body by the guardian, Yaubl Sacabi. In time, you will learn more about this place and of him and his role in the worlds of God. However, right now there is something more important for you to grasp.

Chu-Tay's voice was calming as he spoke assuredly:

"There is a well known equation about responsibility and freedom. The more responsibility we accept, the more freedom we gain. Take for example relationships. The more we do for ourselves and the more we accept responsibility for our lives, the greater the freedom of action we have. After all we have actually created our life by our every thought, word, and action.

No longer do we lay blame for our lives outside of ourselves. We recognize that we have agreed to our upbringing and the circumstances of our life for our personal growth as Soul.

Whatever the process, whether it is health or other difficult circumstances, it is important to take control of it, to take some action and by implication, responsibility. Spiritual freedom is gained when you take charge and search for the answers within. It is manifesting when you rise above the thought patterns of the crowd and when you start to see your life as a creative process.

You two are discovering the importance of seek-ing answers and direction from within, particularly now in your present challenge. This is your key to survival.

Chu-Tay's voice began to fade off as he said, *"Your spiritual destiny is what you wish to create. And what you wish to create lies within your heart."*

In the morning stillness we opened our eyes and looked at each other and smiled. We recognized that we both had been at the golden wisdom temple and had heard the message. Chu-Tay's words, "This is your key to survival," rang in my head and I resolved to continue with the spiritual process that had "led me to her door."

Chu-Tay had a knack for leaving me with unanswered questions, and now I was left with an even greater burning curiosity about Yaubl Sacabi and who he is, and this place that Chu-Tay called Agam Des.

After the Spiritual exercise we were both feeling re-freshed with new energy, and I felt a new determination to survive and create something together with Lena. We had come a long way together in a very short time. I reached into my pack and found an energy bar and water. I broke the bar and gave her half, and then we shared some water.

I said, "Let's keep going for a little while more, until the sun is up."

The trail was wide enough at this point, so I took her hand again, and we walked side-by-side onward and upward over the old overgrown trail, climbing for another half hour through the smells of the morning haze. Soon the sun was up over the horizon and burning the mist off the landscape. I was beginning to recognize some of the ground we had covered yesterday and felt a familiar comfort in seeing the territory again.

Then in the distance we heard a strange sound as we continued our climb. At times it was distinct and then there was silence. I couldn't place it but it sounded somewhat familiar, and ominous at the same time.

Chapter 25
Imagination

The strange sound got louder as we continued our steady climb. I stopped to listen, but it faded away, and then it got louder again. It reminded me of a motor, but kept fading in and out. After a few minutes the sound got steadily more audible and consistent and we stopped to listen.

"It sounds like a helicopter," Lena declared, and I listened some more.

"I think you're right. Let's keep a low profile so we're not seen."

As we rose in altitude climbing up the trail, the vegetation was thinning, and we were losing the benefit of the heavy ground cover. A helicopter could easily spot us if we weren't careful, I thought. Suddenly, the sound was almost upon us as a small helicopter came up over a rise heading directly for us. It was skirting just above the trees, and I got the distinct feeling they were looking for us. We hit the dirt and huddled beneath a bush as the helicopter passed overhead. Lena looked up to see what was happening, and the next thing I knew she was standing up waving her arms shouting, "Papa, Papa."

She had recognized the figure leaning out the window. I was instantly up on my feet beside Lena, jumping up and down and waving my arms to attract their attention as well. As the helicopter banked to complete another scan of the trail area, I could see the figure in the window motion to the pilot. The helicopter stopped and hovered as the man inside waved, and I could see a big smile on his face. The helicopter edged forward and positioned overhead and I felt waves of joy running through my body as the prospect of rescue hovered above. There was no place to land as the terrain was too steep and rough. We didn't know what to do. We stood there for a minute, and then a rope ladder appeared out the side of the helicopter.

"They are lowering a ladder for us!" Lena screamed above the sound of the rotors. My heart was skipping with excitement. The ladder dropped quickly, and I motioned for Lena to grab on and climb up as the helicopter hovered above. She caught hold just as a shot rang out. The helicopter sputtered, and I looked up to see fluid pouring out a hole in the fuselage. Another shot rang out, another hole appeared and the helicopter started to list. Lena looked down at me with terror in her eyes.

I yelled, "Jump, jump!" but she seemed to be frozen in fear. She hung on as the helicopter began to sputter and wobble. "Jump!" I yelled, "It's been hit. It's in trouble." Another shot rang out and I could see commotion in the cockpit. I was desperate. I jumped up and grabbed Lena's leg and pulled. She let go and fell landing on top of me in some brush which broke our fall. We lay there in a heap, terrified at the sounds of the gunshots, and looked up as the helicopter banked steeply out of control. More bullets punctured the side of the cabin as the helicopter disappeared over the rise. Seconds later we heard a terrible crash and could see flames and black smoke rising from a large explosion that occurred just below our line of sight. I hugged Lena as she shook uncontrollably on the ground, screaming, and for a second I had a flashback to what Chu-Tay had said about cycles to our lives and death. The gunmen were not far down the trail, and we were in grave danger.

"Lena, we have to get out of here." I tried to bring her to the awareness that we had to move. I hugged her and shook her at the same time, trying to comfort her but also to bring her out of her shock. I thought to myself, continuing up the trail was useless. We would be exposed. In a minute she began to calm in my arms, and I said to her with a forced authority, "Please be brave. We have to find a way out of here."

She nodded weakly.

"We can't go up the trail anymore," I continued, trying to be positive. "They will see us. Let's try a different tactic. We'll have to crawl so won't be seen. Are you okay to follow me?"

She seemed very out-of-it and in a daze, but nodded again.

I began crawling and looked around to make sure she was following, and she was. I could feel the sharp stones digging into my knees and my hands were feeling them too. I headed down a slope to the other side of the trail away from the crash. I estimated the gunmen would be on us in less than five minutes, so we had to move fast. About twenty feet away from the trail, the slope became very steep, and I turned around so I was facing outward and proceeded down on all fours like a crab. Lena followed suit and we were almost sliding down on our rears when I spotted a crevice. I stopped Lena on the sharp incline, and we slid over to the opening.

"A hiding place," I whispered, knowing that our pursuers could be close now. "We'll squeeze in there." I took her hand, and we laid down flat in the opening. I rolled in and slid down about four feet, landing on what seemed to be a flat surface. I looked up and motioned Lena to do the same. She edged into the narrow opening, sliding on her back, and I helped her down onto the floor. I looked around and discovered we were in some kind of grotto.

We were able to walk upright, and in the sliver of light from the opening we could see that the cave extended into the mountain some distance. I took off my back-pack, reached in and pulled out my flashlight, snapped it on and grabbed Lena's hand as we proceeded to go in. The ceilings were about seven feet high and the cavern was quite wide, about twenty feet. We walked in about fifty steps, and in the beam of my flashlight I saw a ledge along one of the walls. I led her over and we sat down on the shelf and turned off the light.

I put my arm around her in the blackness, and she threw both arms around my neck. I discovered my arm was shaking, and I tried to reposition it a little to stop it. The reality of our situation was now hitting me, too. And I felt a big knot forming in my stomach. It was dead quiet except for Lena's gentle sobs. I didn't know what to say, but I felt we were safe for the moment, just waiting in the dark. Sitting there with arms wrapped around each other, we could see the light of the entrance but nothing moved. My pounding heart began to calm down, and after a few minutes, she stopped crying as well. Trying to reassure her, I whispered, "We're safe here. They won't find us in here."

"Papa came for me and now he's dead." She started crying again, and I held her even more tightly, trying to give her hope, not knowing what else to say.

After about ten minutes, there were no sounds coming from outside our cave. I whispered into Lena's ear, "We need to focus inward. We need to work with Chu-Tay. It's our only way out. Do you think you could sing HU?"

She pulled back and let go of my neck, and I knew she was nodding her head in the darkness. We both straightened around, sitting beside each other and took several deep breaths to calm ourselves a little more. I could hear Lena sing HU just under her breath with her voice trembling, and I joined her whispering as well. In the dead silence of the cave, our faint whispers carried and bounced off the walls creating an ethereal sound, only audible to the two of us.

After several minutes of following the outer sound, I reached a level of calm with my heart beating a normal rhythm. At this point a spiritual sound came to my inner being as the sound of a flute, and then a soft golden light with golden sparkles seemed to envelop the two of us. After another few moments I realized we were with Chu-Tay in the temple of golden wisdom again, and he was smiling at the two of us.

He began to speak saying:

"My heart goes out to you in this moment of immense loss. Life is full of great trials and the most difficult of these challenges can be the loss of loved ones. Please rest assured that there is no finality. There is only transition as we all grow from these life experiences. Soul is eternal and never dies and your father, as the Soul that he is, has passed on and now exists in another Spiritual heaven or plane. It is important for you to focus on this fact in your present circumstances and to maintain balance and be open to Spiritual assistance. All you have to do is look around you.

216

If we imagine ourselves in different circumstances, we can bring these new realities into our life. The key is patience and letting go. We turn the timing and the way our 'imagining' manifests in this world over to Spirit. This will help you in your crisis now."

His words trailed off as the inner light faded, and we were alone in the grotto. I reached out and put my arm around Lena again and whispered, "We are going to be all right. We'll find a way out of this," I said with a new surge of assurance in my own heart. She gave me a kiss and put her head on my shoulder, and I could feel her relax more. I was grateful that she had stopped trembling. e stayed like that for what seemed like about another half hour, listening to the silence. I turned on the flashlight again and found another power bar in my knapsack for us to eat. I broke it in half and then found my water bottle too. We ate and felt good at being safe for now.

Something Chu-Tay had said jumped into my con-sciousness. At the time he spoke the words, they seemed a little out of place and then I lost the thought as I followed the rest of what he was saying. But now the words were coming back to me and I began to feel that he was offer-ing some direction, albeit in a very subtle way. I remember him saying, "All you have to do is look around you."

Chapter 26
The Golden Wisdom Temple

It was starting to feel chilly in the cave. We settled down from the trauma of seeing Lena's father downed in the helicopter and the gunfire from the bandits. Holding Lena close was a good idea to just survive and stay warm, I thought. As I held her, my mind drifted to other things Chu-Tay had also said, and then I began to think about how we were going to get out of this situation.

I got the sudden urge to get up.

"I'm going to look around, Lena. Something Chu-Tay said is telling me to do all we can. Just stay here for a minute. You'll be able to see."

She gripped my arm tightly and whispered sadly, "Be careful, Jack. I don't want to lose you too."

I nodded and stood up and flicked on the flashlight. I walked to the front of the cave to see if the bandits had gone, and if it was safe to leave. As I stood there, to my shock, I could hear voices from outside. A chill went up my spine! I turned around and headed back to Lena, and when I got to her I told her the news. We had to do something! Lena started to shake as I shone the light into the cave and something caught my eye off to the side by the wall. It was a flat rock, and I remembered Paulo telling us to look for trail signs that included cairns and flat rocks.

I left Lena again for a moment and walked over to the far wall by the rock, looking behind it. There was an opening in the floor and rough steps leading down, covered in cobwebs. I went back to where Lena was seated and put on my back-pack. "I have something to show you." I said with enthusiasm. I took her hand, and led her with the flashlight over to the steps. I shone the light down the hole in the floor.

"Want to explore?" I questioned, and she smiled, feeling a surge of hope that there was somewhere to go, something we could do. "Only if you go first," she replied. "I really hate spiders and this looks worse than a horror show."

"Just pretend that you are the Bachelorette and you've chosen me to lead you down these stairs to the stage," I joked, trying to keep the mood light, even though I was really wired and on edge. It looked like we had found a very old Inca passage as I illuminated it once more with my flashlight before taking a first step. Then I proceeded down, holding Lena's hand. I held my hand out in front of me, waving it up and down with the flashlight to push away the cobwebs, and we made our way down through the sticky mess. I didn't want to ask Lena how she was doing, since I was covered in webs and knew she must be too. And I didn't want to think about how large the spiders might be. We picked our way down at least a hundred steps, and as we descended, we began to hear the sound of running water in the distance. As we continued down, the sound gradually got louder and louder. The staircase ended, and I shone the light forward. We were in another cavern, and while we moved along, the sound of the water grew louder as I madly brushed spider webs off my face and hair. I shone the light and could only see blackness. My flashlight was not lighting up anything, it seemed. We continued moving slowly and there, just ahead in the blackness, was inky rushing water; what appeared to be an underground river. We were near a rock edge of the bank. I shone the light along the edge of the bank in the giant underground cavern and the weakening beam of my flashlight revealed something up ahead. We moved along to the edge to the large object. On examination it looked like an upside down dugout canoe under all the dust and webs!

I tapped it and brushed off the cobwebs and dust. Sure enough, it was a native dugout. I looked the canoe over for cracks and it looked all right. It appeared that it could float. "This must lead somewhere," I said to Lena. "This dugout got here, and there must be a way out. This feels good with all the dreams of water that I've had lately."

She nodded and replied in a low voice, "I'm ready. This looks far better than trying to go out the other way." She was standing there still trying to get the rest of the cobwebs out of her hair.

I affirmed, "Let's give it a go."

We both pushed with all of our strength, and the canoe finally moved. Another push and we rolled it over close to the edge. I pushed on the back end and pivoted it over the rock edge of the river bank. Then I said, "You hold it over the water while I push the front end in."

I gave the bow a giant shove, and the canoe splashed into the water.

The current began to pull the boat as Lena struggled to hold it. There were no paddles in sight so I said, "Quick, jump in the back. I'll lead with the light."

Lena was in the dugout in a flash. It was heavy and very stable with her weight. I stepped in, and it was still floating us high and dry by at least six inches, so I pushed us off. I shone the light as we drifted along. We left the cavern after about half a minute and picked up speed as the river narrowed in the huge subterranean chamber. It almost felt like an underground lake where we had found the canoe. Then the ceiling came into site in the beam of the flashlight, and I knew the cavern was getting smaller. We crouched over in the canoe just in case the ceiling suddenly dropped a lot more. It was difficult to tell how fast we were going, as the canoe seemed to move along naturally in the center of the current. We must have floated downstream for at least half an hour when the flashlight started to flicker. The ride was feeling almost leisurely, and I was almost relaxed except for the fact that I hadn't a clue where we were headed. But I felt strangely at ease. I turned around and Lena seemed to be settled down too.

"Lena, I'll have to turn the flashlight off to save the battery." She looked at me expectantly but didn't say anything, so I flicked the switch. In the pitch black. I couldn't even see my hand, and suddenly it was quite unsettling yet at the same time I felt strangely comfortable in the experience, almost like I was reliving it. I was wondering how Lena would react, when she called out in the blackness, "Jack, I'm pretty sacred. Let's sing HU so I can at least hear you."

"Great idea," I replied as

We began to sing HU, and it was a beautiful sound echoing in the cavern along with the sound of water lapping. I felt much better hearing her voice, and knowing she was holding up after all that had happened to her. Soon I was drifting in my consciousness, and I began to hear the sound of tinkling bells. My vision started to fill with a soft blue light, and I felt even more comfortable in the dugout. I focused my attention on the pale blue inner light while also following the inner sound of the tinkling bells. Chu-Tay's face appeared as I became aware of sitting in front of him with Lena at my side in the same golden wisdom temple we visited before.

"Can you tell me more about this place, Chu-Tay?" I asked silently.

"Yes, this is the ancient golden wisdom temple called Gare-Hira, and it is located in the spiritual city of Agam Des in the Hindu Kush Mountains as I mentioned before. The spiritual city of Agam Des cannot be seen with ordinary eyes. It is existent at a higher vibration, and only those that are spiritually mature enough are able to see it and visit here. The name "Agam Des" means "inaccessible world."

There are many other golden wisdom temples in the spiritual worlds, on each spiritual plane and as Soul we are able to visit these places of learning. Usually a visit is by invitation only; by the invitation of a spiritual guide such as I. You are here also with the permission of one of the guardians, Sri Yaubl Sacabi, a Master from the Order of Vairagi Adepts. Along with yet higher entities they form an esoteric group whose existence has been known to mystics in every age. Their purpose is to assist in the advancement of mankind, among other spiritual duties.

There are many golden wisdom temples that can be visited in the Soul body but there is one that can be visited in the human flesh on Earth. This you will discover for yourself when you are spiritually proficient.

When the student is ready, the master will make himself known. You and Lena now know this to be true. When you have reached a certain level of awareness, you are magnetized or attracted to the right teacher to help you move forward. It is a Spiritual principle, the Law of Attraction.

Chu-Tay's words trailed off and I became aware of my singing with the sound of the rushing water. Chu-Tay had given me much to think about, but each time I felt like he was opening up more questions for me. Now I was really curious about the Vairagi Adepts and the other spiritual planes, and the golden wisdom temples. And he said it's possible to visit one in the flesh on Earth!

The sound of the water seemed to be louder than before, so I paused in my thoughts to listen intently. Water was definitely roaring up ahead. I flicked on the flashlight and shone it ahead. To my horror, I could see we were heading into churning water!

"Get ready," I exclaimed. "We're heading into some rapids! Hold on to me Lena—grab my knapsack!"

The canoe plunged into the rapids and under we went. The log canoe seemed to plunge out from under us as we floated above it. The water was icy cold, the same temperature as the waterfall where Paulo and I had rescued Lena, and we both gasped for air with the sudden shock.

Chapter 27
Conquering Stress

Lena was clutching my knapsack, which was still on my back as I battled to keep my head above water. We were being carried down the rapids at great speed and I could feel my legs hit the large rounded rocks below the surface as we were swept down the black passage. The icy water was numbing my legs and hips to the bumping on the rocks, and I could not get the flashlight above the water to see where we were.

All at once it seemed like we were being carried over a small waterfall. Then suddenly we were emptied out into calmer water. I got my hand above water and found the dim flashlight was still on. I shone it around trying to keep my head above water with my other arm, but Lena was dragging on me. I could see we were now in a pool. Over to the side, there was a rock ledge similar to the one we had departed from in the dugout.

Lena was dragging me under, and I gulped some water. I gave my legs a big kick and got my head up above water and gasped, "Lena, let go!" She let go just as my head was about to go under again, and I was relieved to feel the weight lift off my back. I turned around and shouted over the roar of the waterfall, "Swim to the edge!" I paddled with my hands trying not to let go of the flashlight and reached the rock edge alongside Lena.

"Pull yourself up," I sputtered. She began pulling herself out, and I gave her a boost that sent my head under the water again. When I came up I could see she was almost halfway up on the ledge. She managed to get to her knees and she yelled, "Give me your pack!" I wiggled out of it in the water and realized that it had been dragging me down. She grabbed it, and I was boosting myself out before she could grab me, too. The flashlight was flickering, so I shut it off while we lay there exhausted gasping for breath in the pitch blackness. It was incredibly cold, laying water-soaked on the stone. As soon as I caught my breath I stood up and pulled Lena to her feet. I snapped on the flashlight, shone it on her and said, "That was refreshing, and, no more cobwebs." She was pulling her tangled hair away from her face, which bore a fake grin as if to say, "Ha-ha!"

"Do I look like the bachelorette now?" she pouted, shivering.

"No, you look like you just won a reality show contest!" I said, continuing to poke fun at her to keep her feeling positive. "After this, nothing will bother us—I think we're ready for a couples adventure TV show. What do you say?"

"I think we'd better get out of here first!" she retorted playfully, but I knew she meant it.

I shone the flashlight around, looking for a way out and saw a flat rock. My heart started to pound with anticipation! I led her over to it, and the dim light illuminated a staircase leading up, covered with cobwebs as well. Before we could take our first step, the light gave out. In the pitch blackness, I led her up, holding her hand, breaking a path through the webs for us with my free hand. We slowly felt our way with each step, as we proceeded together, with me in the lead, my eyes mostly closed to keep the webs out of them. I counted one hundred and thirty steps, and then they ended. We were on a flat rock surface.

I brushed my hand over my face to clear the webs away and fully opened my eyes. Looking ahead, I could see very faint light. I slowly inched us along toward the light, testing each step before placing my feet down, never sure if we were going to step into a hole or crevice in the cavern. As we moved forward about twenty paces, we could make out the cavern floor we were walking on, and then ahead we could see an opening. We had found the outside! But where were we, I thought?

The exit was overgrown with brush, but we managed to squeeze through, and in a moment we were out in the sunshine. We stood there letting our eyes adjust to the sun which was high in the sky. I had lost all track of time, but estimated it was mid-day judging by the position of the sun and the temperature, which felt to be about seventy-five degrees. The sun felt beautiful as I took off my shirt to ring it out. Lena did the same, and I could not help but notice her athletic body. We found a couple of rocks and laid our shirts in the sun, cautiously looking around. We found a large rock to sit on and soon we were both feeling a lot warmer basking in the sun.

I felt like it would be almost impossible for the kidnappers to follow us now, but I didn't want to take any chances. I looked above into the mountains for a few minutes to see if there was any movement, but there was none. Then I turned on the rock and shifted my attention to the valley below. As I looked down along the valley, I could see a town in the distance at the end of the valley.

"That looks a lot like Agues Calientes!" I exclaimed. "See the train on the main street?"

"I'm sure that's it!" Lena shouted with joy.

"We'll have to stay hidden as much as possible, so let's take another precaution, Lena. Let's cover your hair."

I reached into my knapsack and pulled out a black T-shirt. I rung it out as much as possible and gave it to her. She wound up her long wet bond hair, and wrapped the damp T-shirt around it.

We grabbed our shirts, now partially dried, and put them on without tucking them in so they could dry as we walked. We headed down the mountain slope and picked our way through the brush and grasses. It was relatively easy going compared to some of the other terrain we'd been over. We could see the Urubamba River below and I led the two of us along, gently ascending in a direction that followed the river. Within an hour, we had reached the edge of town, our clothes almost dried in the warm sun, except for my cotton underwear. Thank heavens for quick drying adventure clothing, I thought. We circled around some back streets and lanes, not wanting to be seen, looking for a way into town without having to give away our presence. Glancing down one street I saw part of the train and realized we could catch it as it prepared to leave the station.

I grabbed her hand and said, "Let's make a run for it." We ran to the ticket booth, a block away. I got my wet wallet out and gave the ticket master some soggy bills. He looked at us curiously, but he took them all and gave us the tickets. "Gracias, Senor." He pushed some change back to me through the wicket, but I said, "Keep the change," leaving it for him, and bolted toward the last car with Lena in tow. The conductor's whistle blew as we jumped on board.

We had no idea where we were headed, but I was certain there was only one line out of town, and that was back up the Urubamba river valley towards Cusco. We found seats on the crowded train in the next car, and Lena put her head on my shoulder, still wrapped in the T-shirt. We were both exhausted from our early morning wake-up call, the almost-running trek up the mountain, the shock of the loss of her father, and then the underground waterway "adventure."

Our hearts were still beating with anxiety as the train pulled out of town. We kept a low profile in our seats, looking away from the window. As the train passed the Machu Picchu Pueblo Hotel, I began to relax a little. I whispered to Lena, "I stayed there the first night I arrived. It seems like so long ago now."

"This last week has been a lifetime for me too," she smiled, giving me a gentle kiss on the cheek. I could tell she was starting to relax as well, as the train moved uneventfully out of town. I fought off closing my eyes for a long while, just to be sure we were not going to be surprised once again by the kidnappers. I wanted to make sure we passed by the Chachabamba station without anyone getting on.

Twenty minutes later the train slowed, but did not stop in Chachabamba, and I relaxed a little more. A half hour later as we chugged along into the afternoon sky, with Lena's head on my shoulder, I instinctively began to quietly whisper HU and I could hear Lena join me softly. We soon found ourselves with Chu-Tay in the Gare-Hira Temple, and this time it registered with me that the walls seemed to be glowing of their own accord. Chu-Tay invited us both to sit near the podium, and he was smiling a knowing smile as he began to speak to us.

"The two of you have been through much, but you are learning to handle tension well. In Western society, you call it stress.

Stress is a great teacher. It is actually the opposite of trust, a trust in ourselves and in creation. Stress or anxiety is born out of fear and this fear is a result of not accomplishing what the mind wants or thinks should happen. But the mind is not ultimately in charge here. Soul is. The mind though, has become so important to our survival that most of us have come to rely on our thinking processes and this is the trap. Stress is a condition that is mentally created. It is our reaction to things happening around and to us, and we are spinning out of balance trying to handle too much.

Stress is therefore a trap of the mind based in the fear of not accomplishing what we <u>think</u> we need to do. But what does our heart say? Are we following our feelings? This is our ultimate goal, to follow our heart and to be guided by our higher authority, Soul. Soul really knows what is best and by flowing with Soul, life is a much smoother, less bumpy road. The key is tuning in to Soul and trusting life to our inner guidance.

Knowing this, stress and trepidation can be a great teacher in this regard. When we feel it, we can recognize that we are off course and responding to the mind and its agenda. This is a signal to pause and rebalance with a slowing of the pace and a spiritual exercise. And so once again we come to the ultimate tool for rising above the noise of life, the contemplative spiritual exercises to help you replace stress and its companion, fear, with love

*and joy in your life. Fear cannot exist where love
dwells"*

As he finished speaking, we drifted off into a deep
sleep.

Chapter 28
A Great Spiritual Teacher

I awoke to the sound of the train whistle. The warmth of Lena's body next to mine felt good after being chilled in the underground stream. My clothes were almost dry, and my underwear was drying out as well. My stirring brought Lena out of her sleep, and we looked at each other, then kissed—a long tender kiss. We were both exhausted from the ordeal and feeling the tension of the events of the day, the helicopter crash, the death of Lena's father and the pursuit of the gunmen. And we were very hungry. I reached into my still damp knapsack and found one last soggy power bar. I peeled the wet paper off it, broke it in half and gave her a piece. We still had a little water left as well, and we emptied the bottle.

The train rumbled on into the late afternoon, and I decided to see if anyone could speak English. After approaching people, I found someone who could understand a little and I was able to verify that our destination was indeed Cusco. I returned to my seat to tell Lena the news. She really needed good news, and throwing her arms around my neck, gave me a long hug. She felt so good next to me I didn't want to let her go. With my arm around her shoulders and hers around my waist, we slouched back into our seats. I had learned that it would be about six o'clock in the evening when we'd arrive.

I started singing HU silently again and drifted off into another contemplation. I suspected Lena was doing the same. Soon the inner sound of chimes in the distance began to enter my awareness. I became aware of a brightness in my peripheral vision and it gradually filled my inner sight with a pale yellow light. Chu-Tay's voice entered my consciousness and I could see him as he began to speak. We were with others seated in a semi-circle on the floor around him near the podium in the golden wisdom temple listening to his sonorous voice.

> "As Spiritual Beings we are working towards greater and greater awareness of who we are as Soul and who we are in relation to the Creator. Unfoldment is an eternal activity of Soul. One of the best ways to expand consciously is to begin to serve life. By serving others and all life, we begin to spiritualize our thoughts words and deeds and, in short we are learning to be more God-like.
>
> Help in making our journey can be found through a great spiritual teacher in the spiritual worlds called the Mahanta. This teacher is an expression of the Spirit of God that is always with you and you will recognize him when you are spiritually ready. I serve the Mahanta too and yet I consider the Mahanta to also be my guide.
>
> The Mahanta can also show you the way back home to the heart and center of God."

Chu-Tay's voice faded off as I thought of the word that had already come into my consciousness. I had sung "Mahanta" and seen the blue light! This is the great spiritual teacher, I thought as I felt chills of realization pass through my body in waves!

I opened my eyes and looked up and saw Lena smiling with tears of joy streaming down her face. She had heard Chu-Tay's words too and was as moved as I was.

This was turning into one Spiritual journey, I thought. I wondered what was next, after all we'd been through.

Chapter 29
The Light

The train rolled into the station in the bustling heart of Cusco and we were soon out on the street surveying the scene, not wanting to draw attention to ourselves. Our first imperative was to find a police station, and I thought to myself that there must be one nearby. After walking a block, Lena spotted a plaque on a wall, and indeed it was a local constabulary, so we entered.

An hour later we had given our report of events to an officer that could understand some English. After talking to his commanding officer, he assured us that the police were already in control of the area around Puente Ruinas. He explained that the helicopter crash had led the police to the gunmen and that one had been killed on the mountain side and two others had surrendered and were arrested. These two had led the police to the camp hidden up the valley from Chachabamba where several others had been taken as well, after a gunfight. It turned out that the police had been scouring the mountainsides and valleys by helicopter for the two of us, and they were grateful we were safe and that they were now able to call off the search.

Lena and I completed filling out our report to the police and asked them to make arrangements to have the body of Lena's father returned to Sweden. We were wondering what they would say about our miraculous escape in the cavern through the underground river, but we figured it would be a while before they could read the report we had completed, and we were dead tired and could only think of finding accommodations for the night. We were not anxious to get caught up in unnecessary details, as tired as we were, so we gave the officers our thanks and headed out onto the street, walking along hand in hand and feeling free but drained.

I said, "Let's just get the first decent hotel we see," just as two taxis honked at us, asking if we would like a ride. I opened the door of the first one for Lena, followed her in and I asked for the Posada del Inca, the only inn I could remember, the one where I had stayed before in Cusco. Within a few blocks we were there, near the main square and familiar surroundings. It felt a bit strange, the two of us checking in with just my knapsack, but after all we had been through, I soon dismissed that thought. I ordered room service for dinner at the front desk and then we headed upstairs.

Our room was on the third floor, and my first task was to get all of the clothes out of the knapsack and hung over the shower curtain rod to dry. Then I called down to the front desk for a toothbrush for Lena, and within five minutes, a porter had delivered a little emergency toiletries kit. She was delighted! Lena grabbed the hair dryer and dried her hair, more to warm her head up than to look beautiful. Dinner arrived and we dined overlooking the square of golden floodlit colonial architecture, able to fully relax for the first time in a week.

A half hour later we were in bed in each other's arms, and one long, passionate kiss later, we were both falling asleep from the longest, most action-packed day we had ever experienced.

<u>August 27</u>

Following a beautiful long and peaceful sleep in each other's arms we were up at about eight o'clock. Our clothes were now bone dry. I was able to shave for the first time in days and felt great, and Lena was able to take her time in the shower. We would have to do some shopping as well. It felt so natural being with her in relatively normal circumstances, and I was wondering if she was feeling the same.

During breakfast, I said, "What do we do now, Lena? I was referring to buying clothes for her and other mundane things.

"We should decide a few things, like how many children before we get married, don't you think?" she said playfully. She could see how surprised I was, so she leaned across the table and gave me a big kiss.

"I was hoping you would still feel that way. I love you Lena. I knew it the first time we talked on the mountain side. I could feel it."

"I love you too, Jack. Thank you for rescuing me."

"Well, now that we know where we're heading, let's let some others know what's been happening. I think I had better send an email to Jim, my boss in St. Louis and let him know why I'm not at work. Maybe I'll send my friend Roger a message as well.

Lena said, "I'll also send a message to my office in Chicago. I need some time off to deal with Papa's death and to take care of things regarding his funeral. Mama died five years ago, and I'm all that is left of the family."

"Shall we do some shopping for you today?" I asked.

"I'm all right for now. Do you know what I would really like to do, Jack? Since sitting down for breakfast I have been feeling a very strong urge that we should go back to Machu Picchu, to have one last look, and to get my things at the lodge. Also we can see Chu-Tay too." she smiled.

"I forgot about your things there. Hey, I've got a suitcase there too! I almost forgot, it's been so long. But four hours is a long trip again by rail. Maybe there's another way? Let's check around. I saw a helicopter on a pad just outside the Machu Picchu Pueblo Hotel in Agues Calientes as we went by in the train."

After visiting the front desk and sending our emails, we left the hotel to find a travel office. There were two within sight of the hotel entrance, and we went to the closest, three doors down, and walked in. The middle-aged lady looked up from her desk and smiled. "Buenos dias. Are you speaking English?"

"Yes, we are trying to get to Machu Picchu by air. I remembered seeing a helicopter near the Machu Picchu Pueblo Hotel in Aguas Calientes. Can we take a helicopter there from Cusco?"

"There are several flights each day," she replied. "There is a flight leaving in one hour. It takes only 25 minutes to get there. I can sell you a ticket if you wish. The cost is one hundred and twenty US dollars each way per person."

I reached into my wallet, still damp from the soaking the day before and saw there were only a couple of soggy bills left. I pulled out my credit card. "The ads are true," I said to Lena, and then added for clarity, "You know, don't leave home without it!" Lena broke into laughter, the first time I had seen her really laugh since we were last together back in Machu Picchu.

She whispered, "Money won't ever be a problem now. Since my mother passed away and now with Papa gone, I am the only one left to run the company. I knew someday I would have to return. But I didn't think it would be so soon."

Humm, I thought, I've never been to Sweden, maybe the adventure is just beginning.

We had our tickets in a few minutes. Then picked up my knapsack and checked out of the hotel. We grabbed the first taxi in line out front, and with twenty minutes to spare we were at the heliport that operated next to the airport.

Right on schedule, the converted military, troop-carrying helicopter took off with a full passenger load of Europeans, Japanese and Americans seated facing inwards in two long rows, our backs to the outside walls. Thank heavens for the headphones they gave us, as it was a very noisy bird. We could turn around to see the spectacular views as we soared between the snow capped peaks, generally following the winding Urubamba River.

On disembarking the helicopter, we walked past the Machu Picchu Pueblo Hotel with its red-tiled rooftops, and I pointed out the lush gardens to Lena, suggesting that we take a look in later at the orchids and butterflies. For now, our mission was to recover our suitcases at the lodge up top, so we headed straight into town, following the railroad tracks. We walked hand-in-hand past the now familiar cafes and shops. As we approached the cafe next to the hostel where I first saw Paulo, my attention was drawn to the interior. "There's Paulo!" I exclaimed. I pulled on Lena's hand as I turned abruptly to enter.

"Paulo," I shouted, and he spun around. We rushed toward each other and Paulo and I hugged for a long time as we patted each other on the back. Then it was Lena's turn to give him a hug. We all had tears in our eyes, we simply had no words to express our joy. As we stood there in the crowded café, Paulo was the first to break the silence. "I knew you were safe. I could feel it, but I was sure happy to hear officially from the police." He then turned to Lena. "Lena, I'm so sorry to hear of your father and the helicopter crash."

Lena's' eyes filled with tears again as did mine. All three of hugged, and I felt a bond between us that must have had deep roots in the past. As we slowly let go of one another, Paulo said, "I have a little gift for you I have been saving, knowing we would meet again." He pulled out a little yellow business card and handed it to me. I looked at it and was surprised to see the word "HU" on it in large letters. As I stared at it, Paulo said, "This will connect you to your truth." I could feel the sincerity of his gift, and carefully placed the card in a dry part in the middle of my wallet. I thanked Paulo for all of his help and we explained that we were heading up to Machu Picchu to collect our things. With that we said our farewells.

Ten minutes later, on the other side of town, we caught a bus up to Machu Picchu at the top of the mountain and entered the gates to the site, deciding to get the suitcases on the way down so we would not have to carry them around.

We marveled once more at the extent of the ruins and how this city could have been built at the top of this mountain. I had noted that there were many different kinds of stonework construction. We climbed to the top of the citadel believed to be the astronomical observatory and sat down where we had spent some wonderful moments over a week before. As we held hands I looked at her and knew she wanted to do a spiritual exercise, and so we began to sing quietly.

A few minutes into the contemplation, a vision opened before my eyes. I recognized it as Machu Picchu and I got the impression it was about 500 BC. A spiritual temple was being constructed on the site. As the movie-like scene progressed through time, I was shown that the site remained a holy place for spiritual awakening and attunement with spirit and was gradually expanded with classrooms and lodgings, not unlike a spiritual or religious campus would be built today.

For the first thousand years, by 500 AD, I could see that Machu Picchu had become a major center of political power as well as a center of spirituality. However I got the impression that the pure spiritual teachings were beginning to be corrupted by those seeking power and control. In the next 1,000 years Machu Picchu regressed as a spiritual center, and by 1500 AD it had become essentially a political center based on the power of the corrupted spiritual teachings. The use of black magic to control others was prevalent and the spiritual teachings were basically dead. At this point the culture was in the final stage of decline.

Then Chu-Tay's face appeared and he smiled as he began to speak.
"Now I will reveal for you the mystery of Machu Picchu. Your vision was correct. The greed, lust for

power, and the other moral symbols of decline set the stage for the Inca society to be overthrown by the Spanish. The cycle that this society experienced is not unlike the cycles of all great societies that are uplifted by the appearance of the Mahanta or a spiritual Master that brings enlightenment, imparts spiritual truth, and attracts a following of students.

The students do their best to connect to the same spiritual Light and Sound as the Spiritual Messenger, but over time the teachings of the Master, as passed along to their followers, decline in their spiritual content or truth, and certain rituals enter and eventually become dominant aspects of the teaching. The original spiritual message, the ability of each person to have their own experience of God, becomes diluted and eventually is lost, and instead the priestcraft become the interpreter of the experience of God. It is a slow process whereby the play for power is at first subtle and eventually over the years, becomes total control.

When this occurs, power and the human consciousness have come full circle and the society falls into decline until a Master appears once again to bring God's light into the society. It was I that established the original temple at Machu Picchu, following in a long line of Adepts, that have come to bring the light of God to various societies in the history of the world.

Others in my company include the Master Gopal Das who found the mystery schools of Osiris and Isis and also inspired the Egyptian Book of Dreams in ancient Egypt. St. Paul was key to bringing the *teachings of Jesus out into the world. Quetzalcoatl served Spirit in Central America to lift the consciousness of the pre-Mayan civilization; Milarepa taught in ancient Tibet; the Magi were formed from the teachings of Zoroaster in 600 BC in Persia. Another of our company of Spiritual Masters, Rumi, known in his time as Jalal-ud-Din'l-Rumi, was a Sufi, who studied under Shamus-i-Tabriz. He wrote the Masnavi, meaning inner teachings, a huge collection of books in early 11th century Afghanistan. These are just a few of the Masters that have appeared to lift the human consciousness in addition to the others whose teachings have evolved into religions that are still practiced today."*

His voice trailed off, and I found myself still singing HU atop the astronomical observatory which I now knew was an ancient temple site. Lena and I both had come back to present awareness, and we looked at each other to make sure we had both had the same experience, and knowingly smiled at each other. We got up slowly and climbed down. As I looked up at the site again, an inner voice said "take another look at the pyramid." I stared at it, and then I counted the levels from the bottom to the top. Yes, there were fourteen tiers.

Then it dawned on me. I had read somewhere that there are fourteen levels of spiritual consciousness that are possible to experience in the human body.

"There it is!" I proclaimed to Lena. "The final piece of information in the secret that Chu-Tay just gave us—the secret is in the levels. This has fourteen levels. Each level of the ancient temple is symbolic of this spiritual progression and of our mission to grow in consciousness while still in the physical body!"

She looked up and smiled at me and said, "You're amazing, Jack! And this is truly an amazing place."

"Let's go up to the hut and meet Chu-Tay and maybe he will have some tea and biscuits for us," I said with enthusiasm.

We left the site and headed up the Inca Trail full of excitement and anticipation. We arrived at the *Gate of the Sun*, the famous viewing spot for the sunrise over Machu Picchu and stopped to take in the scene that was becoming so familiar to us. We then left the trail as I had done several times the week before and continued, now climbing up the steep mountain slope to the hut. Upon arriving at the ledge, we both stopped, totally shocked and amazed. There was nothing there. The hut was gone! It had totally disappeared! Not even a stone was there as a reminder of its presence. We both looked at each other and began to look around thinking we were in the wrong place, but it was gone. I said, "Let's just rest here and think about this."

As we sat there looking out over the ruins of the lost city, after a moment Lena began to chant " Mahantaaaaaa", the sound that Chu-Tay had talked about yesterday that was actually the name of the great spiritual teacher. I joined her, and soon the single note of a flute began to enter my inner hearing. Then my vision was filled with an awesome electric blue light with the gold corona that I had seen on just a few occasions, and I began to feel the vibration of the experience lift my body energy. I was enveloped in this sensation for what seemed to be an eternal moment as I felt Lena next to me.

I don't know how long we were bathed in this Light and Sound, but we gradually became aware of the smell of roses and I opened my eyes to see. What filled my vision was an amazing sight. There was a giant column of golden yel-low light pouring down from the sky, enveloping the ancient ruins which in that moment appeared to be fully restored in the light to their original splendor. The center of the column of light focused on the tiered pyramid-shaped temple glis-tening in the light, as if clad in gold. With our eyes fully open, the full majesty of this ancient city and the spiritual temple was revealed to us as we sat there in the light!

The scene gradually faded and returned to its con-temporary state, but we continued to sit, surrounded by the smell of roses. After what seemed to be at least ten minutes, Lena turned to me and said, "Jack I love you so much. Will you come home with me to Sweden? Can we get married there?"

My eyes filled with tears as I kissed her and gave her a big hug. I recalled her vision about not being able to marry me in ancient Machu Picchu when we were with Chu-Tay in the ruins. "Yes," I said, "I would love to. I can't think of any-thing more I would love to do."

"Do you think you would like to help me with Papa's company?" she asked.

And Chu-Tay's words about mastering change flashed through my mind as I thought about my new relationship with Lena and what lay ahead, including living in Sweden!

"Of course, let's continue the adventure together," I re-plied. She threw her arm around my neck and we sat there together, positively enraptured in the moment, in feeling only a complete and total love.

Chapter 30
Epilogue

Lena and I landed safely in Stockholm, then flew north to the city of Ljusdal. Her father's funeral was large and celebrated his life as a bold adventurer in business and in his personal travels. I helped with her father's estate and immediately began to run the company as Chairman of the Board. I kept all of the current management team in place so that I could do what I do best; focus on the big picture and reposition the company in the global economy. Lena and I were married in a spiritual ceremony two months later.

Life with Lena and our children has been a joy, and we will always cherish our time in Peru as the adventure that brought us together and taught us so much. By the way, we heard recently that the Peruvian archeologists still had not found the ancient caverns and waterway that provided Lena and I with our escape, even thought, we had given a very detailed description of the location.

Life and its meaning is constantly unfolding for me as I remain open to all of the possibilities each day. I still marvel at how life can catapult me into new, amazing roles—but I discovered that I have to be willing to let go, and go along for the ride. In my case I had to do my part and grow spiritually, using new tools, but I also had to step aside and let Spirit do Its work at times, too.

As I set about to write this story down I was reviewing my journal notes, and right at the beginning I found a journal entry that didn't make sense. I had written, *"You will find the secret, wrapped in an enigma, found within a mystery."* As I read that entry, it all became so clear. I realized that the *mystery* was my own adventure, discovering many spiritual truths and finding Lena. The *enigma* was the conflicting archeological data that had labeled the temple as an observatory, a later "corrupted" use of the fourteen tiered temple, its true original purpose. The secret, of course, was the original spiritual importance of this ancient city that went far beyond its apparent purpose as a regional spiritual nexus of the Incas. Life is like this too, full of discoveries and awakening to greater wisdom.

Lena and I haven't seen Chu-Tay since Machu Picchu but we are grateful for all he taught us. More importantly, he introduced us to the Mahanta, now our teacher. We do our spiritual exercises each morning and evening together and we see our new guide quite often as a blue light. Lena and I are waiting to meet the Mahanta in our inner explorations the way we had so clearly seen Chu-Tay, but Chu-Tay also had said to us that, "When the student is ready, the Master will make himself known." I now know this is true for each of us.

I hope that your life is filled with love and joy and that by me sharing my experiences, you too can grow and find your truth, and live the life of your dreams too.

May the blessings be....
Jack

Afterword

The Writing of The Messenger of Machu Picchu....A Spiritual Experience

In many ways Jack's journey of spiritual awakening is mine too. I try to see all of life as spiritual experience, and the writing of this book has been no exception for me.

One morning ten years ago I awoke at five am and was drawn to my computer with an urge to write. By about seven thirty I had poured out what became the first three chapters of this spiritual adventure, in complete contrast to my usual non-fiction writing. That was all there was, though, just three chapters.

The next morning the same thing happened. I awoke at five am and was again drawn to my computer. Over the next couple of hours another three chapters were revealed. It was an exciting process because I was discovering the story as I wrote, or shall I say I was the conscious channel for this novel. Each morning for ten days this thrilling story of romance, adventure and spiritual awakening unfolded until it was finished. Yet, some important pieces of the book were missing. Jack's Spiritual guide, Chu-Tay, provides powerful insights to assist him each step of the way. In each chapter he helps him overcome challenges and life-threatening situations, appearing in his inner vision, but these vital messages of wisdom from Jack's guide were unwritten.

A few days later in contemplation I got a nudge—the letters! When I first met my wife Andrea two years earlier, I was inspired to share with her some key spiritual concepts. I had written Andrea a letter each day for a month on a variety of spiritual topics. I went to my file of these thirty letters and found the messages in these letters fit neatly into the chapters of the Messenger of Machu Picchu as the spiritual messages from Jack's guide!

Following an adventure on the Inca Trail and in Machu Picchu to add my personal experiences to the story, and during the numerous edits of the book, I lived all of the lessons that each chapter communicates, and explored in depth all of the spiritual techniques and practices in the book in order to bring it into your hands.

I hope you have moved forward in your spiritual quest in some way after reading the Messenger of Machu Picchu. I know it has certainly changed me over the last ten years!

Life truly is a spiritual adventure......
Bob Switzer

CPSIA information can be obtained at www.ICGtesting.com
Printed in the USA
LVOW052252080113

314899LV00003B/642/P